YOUR GUIDE TO
BETTER
ORGANIZING

DISCOVER THE SECRETS TO BECOMING
MORE EFFECTIVE TOMORROW
THAN YOU ARE TODAY.

Volume 4

OF

THE EFFECTIVENESS GUIDE

BY

EDWARD J. MURPHY

Never STOP Learning!

WHAT OTHERS SAY ABOUT
The Effectiveness Institute

"I highly recommend the books from The Effectiveness Institute as texts for new leaders and a review for seasoned leaders - as a reminder of what they should be doing. These books are unique because they're replete with valuable information that you can actually learn today and use tomorrow. If you want to become absolutely essential to any organization, these books are for you."

- *Dennis D. Cavin*
Lieutenant General, US Army (Retired)
Vice President Army and Missile Defense Programs
Lockheed Martin, Corporate Business Development

"I recommend the books from The Effectiveness Institute because Ed Murphy doesn't theorize; he draws on his extensive experience from many years of service in the US Military and from working as an Executive Coach in Corporate America. His keen insights and practical advice make these books required reading for anyone trying to negotiate the maze of organizational chaos."

- *Lee Lacy*
Assistant Professor
US Army Warfighter Book
Command and General Staff College

"The books from The Effectiveness Institute will help you become more effective at work and in life. They will also help you unlock your potential and direct your team to greater success. I highly recommend these books."

- *Lance Revo*
Principal Engineering Design Specialist
Cyber Security at AREVA NP

I DEDICATE

THIS BOOK

TO

My Friend and Faithful Latter-Day Saint.

Greg Potter

Greg, you are a true friend!

You and Jenney have raised four outstanding children.

You truly exemplify one of life's greatest paradoxes:

"Our legacy story always ends the same -

WE ARE WHAT WE LEAVE BEHIND."

Other Books From
THE EFFECTIVENESS INSTITUTE

Here are the eleven volumes from *The Effectiveness Institute*, one for each Core Competencies of Effectiveness:

VOLUME 1: The Power of FOLLOWERSHIP

VOLUME 2: The Power of DELEGATING

VOLUME 3: The Power of PLANNING

VOLUME 4: The Power of ORGANIZING

VOLUME 5: The Power of COMMUNICATING

VOLUME 6: The Power of PROBLEM-SOLVING

VOLUME 7: The Power of AWARENESS

VOLUME 8: The Power of TRAINING

VOLUME 9: The Power of MOTIVATION

VOLUME 10: The Power of CHARACTER

All the above books are available at *Amazon.com*

Never STOP Learning!

This page is intentionally left blank.

CONTENTS

PREFACE

I'm often asked, "What does the picture mean on the cover of your book?"

This picture is a metaphor for the dilemma young people face when coming from school to the world-of-work.

They're unprepared, do not have the right tools, the right motivation, nor any clue of what's most important to every employer on the planet.

The cover image shows a young man rowing a boat in the fog. If you look closer, you'll notice that the boat is too small for the person in it. You can tell because one side of the boat is dipping so low in the water that it's almost taking on water. You can also tell that he has little experience in a boat because the other side of the boat is way out of the water because his weight is not evenly distributed.

He is also rowing in dense fog. He cannot see where he's going. The further he gets from shore; he cannot turn around and head back because he has no idea from which direction he came.

Finally, since he's not wearing a flotation device, he's assuming he won't have to swim. You know where assumptions take you, right? He is totally unprepared.

He didn't plan his trip, nor is he prepared to deal with the consequences of what lies ahead. He is, or will soon be, lost and at the mercy of nature.

Such is the fate of young workers today.

In today's job market, there's a huge skills gap between graduation and the first day on the job. As a result, young people lack the job skills needed to "hit-the-ground-running" and find themselves in dead-end, menial, minimum-wage jobs, trading time for money just to put food on the table. And it will take them decades before they're effective enough to *add value* to any employer. What a waste!

How do I know that? I know it because I've spent 20+ years of my life as an executive coach, working with hundreds of business executives and small business owners, seeking the answer to this simple question:

Why are some people more effective than others?

What do they think, say, and do that made them more effective?

During that time, I was privileged to work with some of the most exceptional men and women in America. Through their example, I learned the true definition of effectiveness by documenting what they did, how they did it, and most importantly, how they made people feel. What you'll find here is the result of my years of research.

Today, my purpose in life is to help you navigate the world-of-work, maximize your true career potential, and become more effective and successful at work and in life.

ENJOY!

INTRODUCTION

"Organizing is what you do before you do something,
so that when you do it, it is not all mixed up."
- A. A. Milne

This book is about **ORGANIZING!**

***Organizing is your* ability to synergize all your human, physical, and financial resources to consistently produce excellent results.**

Organizing is also one of these eleven Core Competencies of your effectiveness and success at work and in life.

Followership, Delegating, Planning, Organizing, Communicating, Problem-Solving, Decision-Making, Awareness, Training, Motivating and Character.

This book is for everyone in the workforce who reports to another person for their work assignments, including employees working for an employer and small business owners, entrepreneurs, and the self-employed working for customers, clients, or patients.

Simply stated, this book is for you regardless of your occupation, position, or level of authority.

You may not realize that *Organizing* is one the most powerful and underrated transferrable skills in business today.

If you fail to get your act together, know what's going on and coming up, understand the expectations of your boss and organization, know the location and status of your resources (people, physical, and financial), you can easily anticipate the consequences.

This happens because many people don't understand the term *Synergize*.

"To synergize means to combine and use resources to produce an effect greater than the sum of each resource."

As a result, they have no idea how to create and change business systems, scale a business, create playbooks, identify and exploit opportunities, enhance quality, create assessment systems, identify priority activities, align focus and priorities, or manage risk - all of which are addressed in this book.

Without these abilities, you'll be wasting your career sitting on the sidelines, watching others move ahead while wondering why?

I speak from 24 years as a US Army Officer and 20 years as an Executive Coach in Corporate America in Seattle, San Diego, Kansas City, and Phoenix. As an Executive Coach, I was blessed to work with some of America's most successful men and women, including hundreds of business executives, teams, and small business owners.

I documented what they said, did, how they did it, what worked and what didn't. But, most importantly, I documented how they made people feel.

As a result, I learned that the most effective and successful people stood out because they were able to do these two things better than anyone else:

- First, to consistently produce excellent results.

- Second, to add value to those who helped produce those results.

This book will enhance your ability to do both.

The fact is that you may be the top producer, but if you haven't added value to those who helped you, especially your boss, you'll never become effective or successful, period.

What new skills or abilities have you acquired in the last twelve months? What contributions have you made to your current position since this time last year?

And, most of all, what are you doing about it?

This book is unique because it:

- Gives you the most actionable tactics, techniques, and tools needed to consistently produce excellent results.

- Teaches you the best practices used every day by the most effective and successful people in their field, which you were never taught in school.

- Provides you with step-by-step instructions explaining what and how things should be done that you won't find anywhere in academia or Corporate America to help you maximize your true potential.

- Contains everything you want to know about *Organizing*, plus everything you didn't realize you need to know about how *Organizing* enhances your effectiveness and success in business.

I know that by learning, using, and sharing the best practices found here, you'll be well on your way to becoming more effective and successful.

Remember, no matter how good you think
you are; you can always be better.

So, what are you waiting for? You have too much to lose by not taking a more active role in your Professional Development.

When you're ready to *elevate-your-game* to the next level, join us on this incredible *Journey of Discovery*.

Also, if you feel this information could help someone else, please let them know. If it turns out to make a difference in their life, they'll be forever grateful to you, as will I.

Never STOP Learning!

Ed

Founder of *The Effectiveness Institute*
email: ed.murphy77@gmail.com

Stop wishing you were better and do something about it today!

This page is intentionally left blank.

1
THE POWER OF
ORGANIZING

"By failing to prepare, you are preparing to fail."
- Benjamin Franklin

This book will give you a far better understanding of *Organizing*, its definition, importance, and how to do it successfully.

***Organizing is your* ability to synergize all your human, physical, and financial resources to consistently produce excellent results.**

Planning is done by defining positions, jobs, authority, and responsibility; by delineating division of labor, work specialization, chain of command, centralization, structuring, integrating; and coordinating goals and activities to resources to attain objectives.

Here, you'll learn to use the most actionable tactics, techniques, and tools needed to Master the Art of Organizing. As an executive coach for over 20 years, I know what your boss and customers expect, especially when it comes to your effectiveness and success at work.

Effective people know that their ability to organize is critical to their effectiveness and success at work. By learning, using, and sharing these best practices, you'll be well on your way to becoming the one person who adds the greatest value to the team - making you essential.

Also, to make this book easier to understand, I'll be using the term "boss" instead of leader, employer, or customer. I do this because if you're an employee, your boss is your employer. And if you're self-employed or a small business owner, your boss is your customer, client, or patient.

This means that you'll always be working for a boss –
whoever pays you for your products or services.

This also means that you'll always be a follower of
someone – whoever pays you for your work.

So, let's get to work!

Have you ever been in a position of not knowing what was going on in your business unit, missing several important deadlines, being late and unprepared for meetings, not knowing what you needed to know, or being overwhelmed? If so, maybe it's time to enhance your ability to organize.

By starting a New Position

As a new member, this is your first task to complete after you arrive. Do you know who's on your team, what they're doing, and how they contribute to the team's goals? Do you have what you need to do the job? Do you know what's going on and what's coming up?

- A list of all members on your team. Learn their names.

- A structural diagram showing who reports to who.

- A listing of everything for which your unit is responsible.

- Any keys, combinations, or passwords that are part of the job.

- Support getting your email and voicemail systems functional ASAP!

- Any documents, supplies, and equipment that pertain to your job.

- A lunch with each team member to get to know them (Yes, you pay, if you're their boss).

- A listing of all recurring events (weekly, monthly, quarterly, semi-annual, and annual).

- A verbal update on Unresolved Issues (Chapter 25), changes, and assignments accepted and made.

- A visit to all appropriate Line and Staff bosses to get to know them.

- All Standard Operating Procedures, Standards of Behavior, and Mission/Vision Statements.

Refrain from asking for or receiving opinions on the past performance of anyone in your unit. You don't want to prejudge anyone. Let everyone start fresh without any preconceived prejudice (good or bad).

Important Terms and Concepts

What's Span of Control?

Span of Control is the number of people you can effectively lead while consistently producing excellent results and serving your team. Have you ever arrived at a new position and found the current structure not what you needed? Review the organizational chart for your organization and your unit showing all the positions and the members who fill them.

Advanced communications technology can increase your Span of Control. However, if you struggle to consistently produce excellent results, you may want to assess your Span of Control: who reports to whom. In each unit, recognize that your challenges will be different depending on your level within the company.

Do you need a #2 Person?

Can you remember when you needed a decision or had a question, and it took hours, if not days, to get a response from your boss because he was gone? How did that make you feel? If your boss had a #2 person you could go to for approval or answer your question, would that have helped you?

It's smart to have a second-in-charge that has full authority to act in your absence. If you're the only one who can make simple decisions, and you're not available, your entire unit comes to a halt. This also applies to your meetings. If you're late or detained with your internal meetings, instead of having all your members standing around waiting for you, your #2 Person can take the meeting, starting no more than five minutes late, and brief you later. Likewise, if you are not available with your external meetings, your #2 Person can attend, take notes, and brief you upon your return.

The important issue here is that your unit must continue to function seamlessly when you're not there. Also, compare vacation schedules with your #2 Person to ensure you're both not absent at the same time.

What do Line and Staff mean?

Here's a Line and Staff structure diagram using a grocery store:

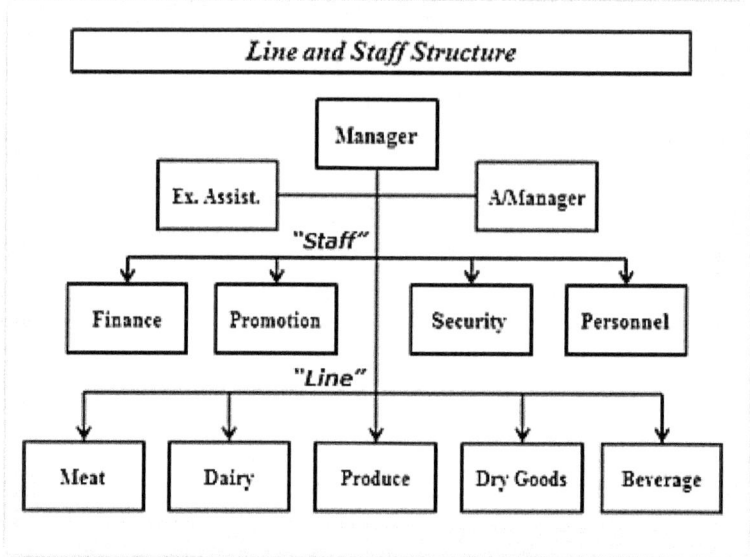

- **The Line structure** interacts with the product and serves the customer directly, and runs from the store manager to the heads of each department within the store like Meat, Dairy, Produce, Dry Goods, and Beverage.

- **The Staff structure** exists to serve the line departments and runs from the store manager to the heads of each staff section within the store like Finance, Promotion, Security, and Personnel.

Some Line and Staff organizations have the rule that a Staff boss can't say "No" to any legitimate request from a Line boss. Only the Store Manager can say "No." However, both Line and Staff units must work together to keep the store running smoothly.

2

BY KNOWING WHAT
COMPANIES NEED TO SURVIVE

"It is the men behind who make the man ahead."
- Merle Crowell.

Do you know what's most important to the survival of every company?

Have you ever tried to figure out what was most important and what wasn't, especially when there were too many things to do and too few people and hours in the day to get it all done?

As an Executive Coach, I often asked senior executives, *"What matters most to the survival of your company?"*

The first answer I normally got was *People*. And people are an important resource, but not the most important resource. Just quit your job and see how quickly you'll be replaced. Some said *Technology*, which is important, but again, not the most important. So, what really matters most?

The only people who don't struggle with this question are the self-employed and Small Business Owners. These guys get it.

They'll tell you that the most important thing to any company is Positive Cash Flow (or PCF).

The company can't pay their people without PCF, and they're soon out-of-business - game over! According to the Small Business Administration, this is the reason 80% of start-ups fail within their first three years.

But what about your business unit? If you can link what you do for your company's *PCF* and how it has improved or achieved better results, your business unit is *essential* to your company.

In the same vein, if you can't be directly linked to one or more of the activities that generate *PCF*, you could be considered *non-essential* and therefore *expendable* - not a place you want to stay for long. So, what activities generate *Positive Cash Flow?*

What activities generate Positive Cash Flow?

- **Increase Revenues:** To increase revenues normally involves sales, marketing, sales support, business development, or strategic development. For example, can you find new and innovative ways to sell more products or services, like bringing in new customers, selling more to the same customers, discovering new uses for old products, and finding new ways to bring more money in the door? This is how revenues are increased.

- **Decrease Operating Costs:** To decrease operating costs, or save money, is everyone's job. Can you find and recommend new and innovative ways to reduce costs like consolidating, eliminating, cost-sharing, getting a better price from a supplier, conserving, saving time, or being more effective, efficient, and consistent? This is how Operating Costs are decreased.

- **Better use of available resources:** Everyone's job is to better use the resources they already have. Can you find new and innovative ways to better use the resources your company already has, like streamlining, eliminating redundancies, consolidating, conserving, waste reduction, process improvement, reducing the time required, becoming more efficient, doing more with less, better-maintaining equipment, and vehicles to extend their service life, and finding quicker or easier ways of doing things? How much money or time could be saved annually? This is how to better use the resources of your company, which saves money.

- **Protect the company by anticipating problems today to save money tomorrow:** Anticipating problems today to save money tomorrow is also everyone's job. Since lawsuits are expensive, can you find ways to anticipate problems today to save money tomorrow, like creating important policies and procedures, creating better contracts, ensuring the right insurance is in force, ensuring compliance with outside agencies, creating better physical and cybersecurity procedures, creating better property accountability procedures, or eliminating unsafe conditions? This is what saves money tomorrow by anticipating problems today.

What matters most to the survival of
Private-Sector Companies like Microsoft?

The *Private-Sector* is the part of the economy owned by private groups and is created to generate a profit. Their focus is on *Positive Cash Flow,* so they don't go out of business. It employs workers through individual business owners, corporations, or other nongovernment agencies. This includes companies like financial services, law firms, newspapers, aviation, hospitality, or other nongovernment positions that maximize their profitability.

What matters most to the survival of
Public-Sector Organizations like Public Schools?

The *Public-Sector* is the part of the economy, which provides a service to the public to help improve their quality of life, livelihood, and the betterment of the community, rather than profit generation.

However, their focus is also on *Positive Cash Flow,* so they can continue to receive the funding needed to pay their employees. This includes organizations like public schools, the military, police, fire, and public works.

Funding for some organizations comes from city, state, and federal tax revenues. Others receive funding through grants or donations. Regardless, all *Public-Sector* Organizations must maintain *PCF* to continue to operate.

The bottom-line is that Positive Cash Flow is the life blood of all businesses regardless of their sector.

This page is intentionally left blank.

3
BY KNOWING WHAT
BOSSES NEED TO SURVIVE

"It takes half your life before you discover
life is a do-it-yourself project."
- Napoleon Hill

Every boss needs effective followers who can resolve problems and achieve goals. And any effective *follower knows how to turn any assignment (a problem, goal, event, or activity) into a simple project and manage that project to a successful completion.

As far as your boss is concerned, your effectiveness or value-added is a function of your ability to successfully manage projects. And you don't need to be a *certified project manager* to manage projects successfully. All you need is a basic understanding of a few tactics, techniques, and tools, which you'll learn here.

The better you get at managing projects, the more value you bring to your boss. And for every project, you'll encounter obstacles along the way. All you need to do is to convert each obstacle into another project and make it go away.

Your effectiveness in the eyes of your boss requires that you satisfy these two conditions:

- To be able to consistently produce excellent results.

- To be able to add value to all those who help you produce those results-including your boss.

And to meet these two conditions requires that you successfully manage projects. Let's address the basics first.

What's a Project?

I define a project as an assignment that requires the effort of others. Anything you can do yourself is a task and not a project. So, whenever you get stuck at work, realize there's a simple way to re-frame anything into a project to get things moving again.

*To learn more about **Followership**, available at **Amazon.com,** see page 5.

What's a Plan of Action?

Every project needs a good *Plan of Action*, even if it's only a mental plan or a sketch on the back of a napkin. Any good *Plan of Action (POA)* format (Appen A) has at least six components:

Objective: Who, What, Where, When, and Why (Appen A)?

Methods: How will we accomplish this Objective (Appen A)?

Timetable: Planning backward from today, how will we use the time available to plan and prepare (Appen A and Chaps 6-7)?

Resources: What will you need (Appen A)?

Unresolved Issues: What are all the things (questions, unknowns, concerns, shortfalls, obstacles, or problems) that could slow or stop your progress (Appen. A, Chap. 16)?

Risk: What could *reasonably-go-wrong* and how can they be *mitigated* (Appen A and Chaps 24-29)?

If you don't know certain information, still list the category, but show a TBD (To Be Determined). For example, if you don't know the end time, show, End time: TBD.

What's a Project's Life Cycle?

Every project has at least four phases: Planning, Preparing (before), Executing (during), and Assessing (during).

Here's a *Gannt Chart* showing the four phases of a one-day project that begins in 30-days:

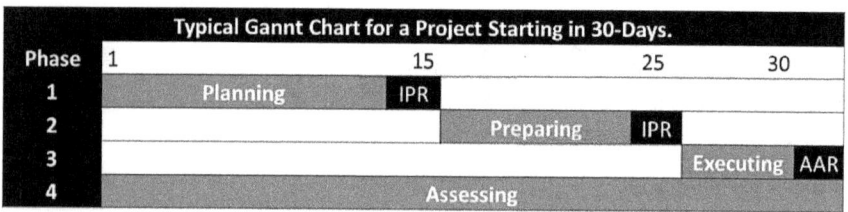

Notice that the *Assessing Phase* is conducted continuously throughout the project and is formalized using two *In-Progress Reviews* (or IPRs) (Chap 29), numerous *Project Updates* (not shown) (Chap 13), and one *After-Action Review* (or AAR) (Chap 34).

4

BY USING
PREVENTIVE ACTIONS

"The policy of being too cautious is the greatest risk of all."
- Jawaharlal Nehru

How do you find problems, or do you wait until they find you? Do you know how to uncover and resolve anything that could slow or stop your work?

Preventive Actions are all the things you should be doing 30, 60, or 90 days before any project to uncover all Pre-Problems.

This process is designed to find and correct any Pre-Problems before they get in front of your boss or the customer.

Pre-Problems include mistakes, defects, shortfalls, omissions, errors, or anything else that could slow or stop your work.

Here are the 20 most important *Preventive Actions* that should be added to your *Project's Timetable*.

THE PLANNING PHASE

1. Conduct an initial Site Inspection:

Visit the site to see if it meets your requirements. If you're asked to select the best site, visit several sites and present the best to your boss. Then, gather sufficient information (like photos, dimensions, and sketch maps) to help you create your *Draft Plan of Action* (Appendix A) and prepare for your *Backbriefing* (Chapter 22). When picking the best site, the most important issues are location, availability, accessibility, cost, and amenities.

2. Create a Draft Plan of Action (POA):

This is your project *Plan of Action* (POA) that includes an Objective, Methods, Risk, Timetable, Resources Needed, and Unresolved Issues. (Appendix A).

3. Identify and eliminate all Unresolved Issues:

What are all the questions, unknowns, concerns, shortfalls, obstacles, or problems that could slow or stop our progress (Chapter 25)? Each issue can only be eliminated when it's both *"known for certain"* and *"acceptable to you."*

4. Anticipate the Unintended Consequences:

What are all the adverse outcomes (*Unintended Consequences*) that aren't expected by your actions (Chapter 26)? Work hard to find anyone who has done this or a similar project before. What problems, consequences, and effects did they have?

5. Anticipate the Second and Third-Order Effects:

What are all the ways your project could affect others at different levels in your company (Chapter 26)? Work hard to find anyone who has done this or a similar project before. What problems, consequences, and effects did they have?

6. Conduct a Risk Assessment:

With your team's help, assess the risk of any safety, security, financial, and operational risk associated with the project and how they can be mitigated (Chapter 32).

7. Conduct a Backbriefing:

This is a briefing given by the Project Manager to his boss explaining how he intends to accomplish his boss's objective. This briefing enhances mutual understanding and trust by exchanging questions and answers to identify any unmet expectations or hidden surprises (Chapter 22). Brief your boss using the *Plan of Action Checklist* (Appendix A). Then, set the schedule for periodic *Project Updates* (Chapter 23).

8. Create a Memorandum of Record:

Finally, create a memo documenting the questions and answers from the *Backbriefing* and any questions you couldn't answer. Ensure your boss and all Key Players get a copy. A Key Player is anyone who must perform a task for a project to achieve its objective.

9. Provide Advanced Warning:

This is informing all Key Players of what's coming, so they can plan. Provide a copy of your Draft POA and the memo from the *Backbriefing* to each Key Player (Chapter 22).

10. Create Contingency Plans:

This plan is executed only if something bad happens that was anticipated, like bad weather (Chapter 35).

11. Staff the POA:

Circulate your POA through all Key Players for their concurrence or non-concurrence with comments (Chapter 27)

Conduct a Decision Briefing: Optional

Conduct a final briefing to the Decision Maker, with all Key Players present, to obtain final approval, if needed (Appendix C).

12. Conduct In-Progress Review (IPR 1):

Conduct at least two meetings before your project to synchronize all Key Players (Chapter 29). IPR 1 should be conducted at the mid-point of the time remaining between the Planning and Preparation Phases.

THE PREPARATION PHASE

13. Conduct Project Update Briefings:

Conduct a briefing to your boss summarizing the status of your project (Chapter 23).

14. Prepare to take Immediate Action:

This is a disciplined drill used to react to bad situations that could cause a work stoppage, property or equipment damage, a security breach, or physical injury (Appendix B).

15. Conduct a Final Site Inspection:

Conduct a last inspection of the project site to see if anything has changed since the initial inspection.

16. Conduct In-Progress Review (IPR 2):

This is a second (or final) meeting conducted 5 to 7-days before the project to confirm that all assigned tasks have been completed as planned (Chapter 29) between the Preparation and Execution Phases. This is when the rehearsal schedule should be distributed.

THE EXECUTION PHASE

17. Conduct Rehearsals:

This is your last chance to see, practice, or test everything before the project to identify and correct any *Pre-Problems* (Chapter 4).

18. Conduct Pre-Staging:

This is the storage of equipment and supplies at the site before a project to make setup easier.

19. Conduct Site Set up:

Set up your site as planned. Having a site diagram (with extra copies) is a good idea – showing where everything goes.

Project Starts:

Supervise all Key Players to ensure the project achieves the desired objective. If problems arise, either execute *Immediate Action* (Appendix B) or a *Contingency Plan* (Chapter 35) to keep the project moving.

Conduct Site Clearing:

This includes all the actions taken after a project. The site may need to be cleared quickly to allow the next user to come in and stage their equipment.

THE ASSESSING PHASE

The Assessing Phase is conducted continuously throughout the project and is formalized using at least two *In-Progress Reviews* (or IPRs), several Project Updates (not shown), and an *After-Action Review* (or AAR).

20. Conduct an After-Action Review (AAR):

Conduct an informal meeting at the end of every project day and the day after the project with all Key Players present to focus on what happened vs. what was supposed to happen. Ask, *"What did we learn that can make us better next time?"* Add the *Lessons Learned* to the *After-Action Report* (Chapter 37).

Conduct Project Close-out:

This includes all close-out details, like administering surveys, paying bills, sending letters, filing the *After-Action Report*, and other details.

5
BY USING A
PROJECT TIMETABLE

Time and tide wait for no man."
- Geoffrey Chaucer

How do you keep track of the important tasks, preventive actions in their proper sequence, and who's responsible for each to help you keep track of what's important (Appendix E)?

A Timetable is a simple table designed to show all the important tasks, their proper sequence, and who's responsible for each.

Your *Project's Timetable* should also contain all the *Preventive Actions* you'll need to manage your project.

Here's an example of a partial project timetable.

Partial Timetable for Company Picnic (June 21)							
Yr	M	D	Time	Preventive Action	Responsible	Where	Who
14	5	2	1 PM	Site visit conducted	Bob	B	1
14	5	4	2 PM	Backbriefing	Bob	A	2

Notice that this table shows the date, time, the *Preventive Action*, the person responsible, the location, who else is involved, and the correct sequence for each action.

The sequence is important because **Murphy's Law** states that:

"Whenever attempting to do anything, there are always things you should have done first."

What did you forget?

Which *Preventive Actions* will you add to your *Project's Timetable* to catch all the *Pre-Problems* before your project starts?

What if you don't know the dates yet?

Here's an example:

> *Bob was having lunch with Joe (one of his Direct Reports) and asked about an important project for his boss. Joe said, "I'll start working on the POA when the company decides on a start date." Bob asked him why he was waiting.*

*Joe responded, "How can I write a POA when I don't know when the project starts?" Bob was stunned! He told Joe that the project starts every year in April, and today was January 1ˢᵗ, so he only had three months to plan. After lunch, Bob guided him through the creation of a Timetable using **S-Day as the Start Date**. Bob also asked Joe to add the most appropriate Preventive Actions to his Timetable.*

Here's an example of Joe's partial *Timetable*.

Partial Timetable for _____ Project (as of Date)							
Yr.	M	D	Time	Preventive Actions	Responsible	Where	Who
15	4	S-7	TBA	Final IPR	Joe	A	2
15	4	S-2	TBA	Rehearsals	Joe	A	2
15	4	S-1	TBA	Equipment pre-staged	Sam	B	2
15	4	S-Day	TBA	Project Starts	Joe	B	1
15	4	S+1	TBA	After Action Review	Joe	A	2

Notice that this Timetable uses **S-Dates** instead of calendar dates because the project's start date has not yet been announced.

Joe then created a POA around this Timetable and began the Planning Phase. He labeled anything in the POA he didn't know for certain as TBA: To Be Announced. He then provided Advance Warning to all Key Players by giving them a copy of his draft POA. When the actual start day was announced, he plugged in the dates, notified all Key Players, and continued the Preparation Phase. If Joe had waited until the date was announced, several Key Players would have been in the last-minute crisis management mode.

Note: In the absence of instructions, make the assumptions needed to move the work forward (Appendix D).

If you fail to include *Preventive Actions* in your *Project's Timetable*, expect to experience the adverse effects of *Murphy's Law*.

6
BY USING AN
ASSESSMENT SYSTEM

*"Don't tell your problems to people: eighty percent don't care;
and the other twenty percent are glad you have them."*
- Lou Holtz

How do you find problems, or do you wait for them to find you?

**An Assessment System is a combination of targeted,
proactive procedures designed to identify problems before
they occur and resolve problems once identified.**

This system is called CAPA (Corrective Actions, Preventive Actions) and
should be part of your overall Quality Management System (QMS) and
includes procedures to prevent problems (PA) and procedures to correct
problems (CA) once identified.

*Mistakes or defects are not a problem if they're identified
and resolved before your boss or customer discovers them.*

By Using Preventive Actions

**Preventive Actions are a series of specific
procedures designed to identify pre-problems before
they get in front of your boss or the customer?**

Pre-problems include anything that could slow or stop the achievement of
your goals (Chapter 4). What procedures do you have to identify problems
BEFORE they get in front of your boss or the customer?

- Do you have processes, procedures, tests, rehearsals, inspections, visits, or assessments?
- Do you need periodic inspections, rehearsals, visits, or assessments to catch defects and mistakes?
- Who's checking, and what are they checking for?
- How often and to whom do they report?
- What do they do when a problem is identified?
- Who's checking the checker?

Corrective Actions are a series of specific procedures designed to respond to problems AFTER they've been identified.

What procedures do you have to correct problems after they have been identified?

What's the Essence of a Finding?

Here's a system to capture, track, and resolve problems:

- **Problem #2214:** for tracking .

- **Standard:** What is the standard?

- **Condition:** What problem was found or observed?

- **Cause:** What is the root cause of this problem?

- **Risk:** What's our Risk?

  ✓ *Impact:* How <u>serious</u> will this problem affect the project?

  ✓ *Probability:* How <u>likely</u> is this problem to happen?

- **Recommendation:** What needs to be done to mitigate or eliminate the root cause?

- **Action:**

  ✓ Who is the *Point of Contact (POC)* to find a solution?

  ✓ When and how is the report rendered?

  ✓ What is being done to correct the problem?

  ✓ What is the current situation – same or worse and why?

Remember, mistakes or defects are not a problem if they're identified and resolved before your boss or customer discovers them.

What do sports teams use?

The day after the game, they all watch the game video. They document and record what happened. Then, they review the entire game, play by play. Did each play accomplish its goal? Did every team member do their job? If not, what needs to be done to improve for the next game?

7
BY UNCOVERING
ALL EXPECTATIONS

"Exceed your customer's expectations. If you do, they'll come back over and over. Give them what they want - and a little more."
- Sam Walton.

The fact remains that you could be the most talented person on the planet, but if you don't understand and meet all the expectations of your boss, company, and industry, you're doomed to failure.

An expectation is a belief that's centered on the future.

A less than expected result gives rise to the emotion of disappointment. If something happens that's not expected, it causes the emotion of surprise. And trust me when I say bosses don't like surprises.

Expectations focus on the desired performance for both results and behavior. To become more effective, you must understand all that's expected of you.

Here are the three most important expectations in the workforce:

By identifying All Stated Expectations

Stated expectations are written and verbal expectations from your boss, job description, and company policies and procedures.

Here are the most important steps to identify all your stated or written expectations:

1. Know your duties.

Your duties are the tasks your boss needs you to perform and are normally found in your job description.

2. Know your responsibilities.

Responsibility is an obligation to satisfactorily perform a task assigned by your boss, which has a penalty for failure and is normally found in your job description. Accepting complete responsibility for what you say and do (and what you fail to say and do) and the consequences are the first step on the path to peak performance and effectiveness.

3. Know your Constraints.

Constraints include imperatives and restrictions.

- **Imperatives** are things you must do (like achieving your goals).

- **Restrictions** are things you must not do (like not accepting gifts from vendors) and include borders and limits.

    ✓ **Borders** are official or unofficial lines dividing one area from another, showing who's responsible for what.

    ✓ **Limits** are the point at which something ends or beyond which something starts.

4. Know your level of Authority.

Authority is your boss's permission to take certain agreed-upon actions on her behalf in support of your official duties and responsibilities.

Authority, unlike responsibility, can be given to another person to perform a specific assignment. When you ask someone to perform an assignment, you're giving that person your authority to act on your behalf. Authority can include making work assignments, hiring and firing, making decisions, or spending money.

So, when you ask someone to perform an assignment, be clear on what they can and cannot do. Also, do you have the authority you need to perform your duties and responsibilities? If not, speak up!

5. Know your Projects.

Do you know all the past projects completed before you arrived, your current ongoing projects, and your future projects coming up soon? A project is any assignment that requires the effort of others, like an activity or event.

6. Know the Standards.

Standards are the established norm or required minimum level of conformity to industry and company policy, criteria, methods, processes, and practices for your results and behavior.

To find the standards that apply to you, review all company guidelines, policies, standards of conduct, and behavior, along with any Standard Operating Procedures. Pay particular attention to safety, security, proprietary information, and intellectual property. This is especially important if you're changing jobs or getting a new boss.

By identifying All Inherent Expectations

If you're responsible for the performance of others, you have another type of duty or expectation.

Inherent duties or expectations are bosses only duties expected And performed by all bosses that cannot be reassigned.

Here are the most important boss-only inherent duties or expectations that will consume 90% of the boss's time:

- Traveling and attending meetings he must attend.

- Conducting internal meetings and following through.

- Briefings those he must brief.

- Responding to emails, voicemails, and other correspondence.

- *Delegating actions and problems to team members to resolve.

- Training members on how to complete projects.

- Solving problems only he can resolve.

- Conducting interviews, checking, and inspecting.

- Planning, organizing, building teams, training, *delegating, and setting goals and priorities.

- Enforcing standards, correcting, counseling, reprimanding, retraining, and punishing.

- Inspiring, motivating, praising, encouraging, consoling, challenging, coaching, and promoting.

As you consider these boss-only inherent duties, realize they're the most important things every boss must do.

*To learn more about *Delegating*, available at **Amazon.com,** see page 5.

Hidden expectations are things that others expect you to do that are either unclear, unspoken, or unwritten.

These expectations are the most dangerous because they lead to poor performance, mistakes, and failure (Appendix J).

For any boss to have faith in you, the issue always involves your performance (your results and behavior).

- Your **results** involve your ability to consistently produce excellent results.

- Your **behavior** involves how well you add value to all those who helped you achieve your results, especially your boss.

If your boss's expectations are hidden or unclear, your performance will suffer along with your credibility, job security, and career. Meeting all your boss's expectations will put you way ahead of your peers.

Here are the most important steps to uncover hidden expectations.

Step 1. Assume nothin!

Be careful with your assumptions (Appendix D).

Step 2. Meet with your boss and ask these questions:

- What's your mission, intent, purpose, and direction?

- What're your goals, values, focus, and priorities?

- What're your expectations of me at your meetings?

- What reports or updates do you expect from me?

- How will you assess my performance for both results and behavior?

- Do I have permission to voice my honest opinion, behind closed doors, without the fear of negative consequences?

- What're your expectations of me for tradition and culture?

- Do I have access to information sharing and processing?

- How do my goals relate to yours?

- What's my Authority to make work assignments, hire, fire, make decisions, or spend money?

- What're my *Imperatives* (things I must do) and *Restrictions* (things I must not do)?

- What're my ongoing and upcoming projects, and which is most important and why?

- What are all the recurring events or activities that occur weekly, monthly, quarterly, or annually?

Step 3. Ask your team members and peers.

Ask them for any hidden expectations. Ask about your boss's idiosyncrasies, strengths, and weaknesses.

Step 4. Ask your predecessor.

Ask about any hidden or unstated expectations.

Step 5. Ask Human Resources.

Ask about any hidden or unstated expectations for culture and tradition.

This page is intentionally left blank.

8
BY CREATING A
READINESS REPORT

"I will prepare, and someday my chance will come."
- Abraham Lincoln

Do you know how to ensure your business unit is ready to accomplish its purpose?

Readiness is the ability of a business to accomplish its purpose.

Any monthly *Readiness Report* starts with the purpose of the business.

The purpose of any business is to accomplish its mission.

Once you have your purpose, the next question is, what's needed to accomplish that purpose? Since this is a monthly report, the next question is what people, vehicles, and training are needed to achieve that purpose?

- **People:** Shows the number of positions *authorized vs. the number of members filling those positions as a percentage.

- **Vehicles:** Shows the number of vehicles authorized vs. the number of vehicles **operational, as a percentage.

- **Training:** Shows the number of members authorized vs. the number of members who have completed all training as a percentage.

---

*Authorized means the number your boss has deemed sufficient for you to accomplish your purpose.

**Operational means the ability of a vehicle to perform its intended purpose.

The goal is to be as close to 100% in all three categories. If not, there should be an explanation on the report of what needs to be done to improve the situation. All unit managers should provide a monthly *Readiness Report* to their boss to assess his unit's readiness.

Note: This may be the shortest chapter in this book, but if you're the boss of a medium to large organization, this is one of the most important.

This page is intentionally left blank.

9
BY ON BOARDING
NEW MEMBERS

"The first day, week, and month of an employee's
experience carries a lasting impression."
- Scott Weiss

How are new members integrated into your business? The terms used here
may differ from company to company. However, the two processes of In-
Processing and Transitioning new members and Direct Reports (DRs)
apply across the board.

How effective is your In-Processing Program?

**In-Processing is the process of orienting and training new
members concerning a company's history, traditions, policies,
procedures, and cultural expectations.**

Should every new member be assigned a "Sponsor"? Absolutely! Have
you ever joined a new company where it took you weeks, if not months,
to find out where everything was or how certain things got done? If you
had a Sponsor to show you around and answer your questions in your
first week, would that have helped you?

The Sponsor's job is to ensure the new person is properly welcomed,
introduced, and successfully in-processed into your unit. Develop your
checklist so that your Sponsors have a better idea of what their duties
include. This process helps the new person assimilate more quickly,
accelerate their learning curve, and feel more like a valued team
member.

Do you have an In-Processing Checklist?

As a minimum, here are the important things you may want to add to
your *In-Processing Checklist.*

*Food, drink, restrooms, hours of operation, meet everyone, learn
everyone's name and function, keys, passwords, phone, program
voicemail, security, badges or passes, do's and don'ts, recording
your time, using organizational software, hours of operation, what's
proprietary, breaks, Standard Operating Procedures, benefits,*

orientations, training, duties, responsibilities, constraints, standards, projects, rules, processes, procedures, parking, supplies, fax, copies, how to contact your sponsor and boss, your phone #, email address, how to dial an outside line, mandatory readings, holiday schedule, Paid Time Off, key terms and definitions, acronyms, chain of authority, and useful URLs.

Note: Some companies assign a sponsor during the transitional process.

How effective is your Transitioning Process?

Transitioning is the process where a boss welcomes and orients a new Direct Report into their team is normally done after they've completed In-Processing.

This section of this chapter assumes that one of your Direct Reports is about to leave your team. Your first problem becomes finding a suitable replacement.

What's the best way to find a new Direct Report?

If you don't have all your Direct Reports to fill your authorized job positions, consider:

- Promoting someone from within your unit.

- Selecting someone from within your company.

- Asking for referrals from your team members.

- Asking for referrals from within your company.

- Asking for referrals from family, friends, and associates.

- Last resort: Create a Job Requisition, which could take several months.

What should the boss do BEFORE a new Direct Report (DR) arrives?

Ideally, it's best to have both the new and the departing DR's transition together before the departing DR leaves. However, this rarely happens. The next best solution is to have the departing DR transition with their boss.

As such, here are the most important steps the boss can take to conduct a good transition or hand-off:

- Before the departing DR leaves, meet with him and discuss the Transiting Process.

- Capture all their uncompleted assignments from their Playbook (see Chapter 16).

- After identifying all past, current, and upcoming assignments, they'll need to be transitioned to you.

- Their Playbook should contain all their assignments, including their POAs, AARs, and any follow-up or follow-through actions that still need to be conducted.

- If the departing DR does not have a Playbook, create a folder of all important documents needed so the boss can conduct a good transition with the new DR after arrival.

What should the boss do AFTER the new Direct Report arrives?

Before your current DR arrives, a *Playbook* should be created for the new DR (see Chapter 16). If the new DR did not come from within your company, ensure he completes the In-Processing Program first. Then, schedule a Transition Meeting. This is your chance to build a relationship and put a face to the name. It's your first impression – make it count!

Here are the most important things to cover during a Transition Meeting:

- How their job fits into your unit (Direction).

- How their job contributes to your goals (Direction).

- Why their job matters (Purpose).

- Any expectations for tradition and culture.

- Give him his *Playbook* and explain its purpose (Chapter 16).

- Discuss your *Serving Philosophy* revealing what you expect from him and what he can expect from you.

- The limits of his authority to make decisions, spend money, make changes, take the initiative, and hire and fire.

- Your meeting rules and expectations of his performance.

- Your intent, responsibilities, expectations, projects, goals, standards, values, and priorities.

- His access to information sharing and processing.

- Your permission for him to voice his honest opinion, behind closed doors, without fear of negative consequences.

Note: Ensure he understands that if he has questions, ask!

At the end of the meeting, ask these questions:

- Do you have a clear picture of what's expected of you?

- What are your assigned duties?

- What assignments are ongoing, incomplete, and upcoming?

- How can you contact the departed DR if you have further questions?

- What are Unresolved Issues, and how are they eliminated?

Once all questions have been answered, the transition is complete, and the new DR is now *in-charge*. These steps, if done consistently, will ensure a more effective and productive transition for your new DR.

Remember, the only stupid question is the one you're too afraid to ask. Because later on, when you don't know the answer, you'll look stupid or worse.

Note: During your first 90-days, there's an unwritten rule that says that during this period, you can ask any question, make any statement, forget any name, or make any mistake. It's like having a free pass for 90-days. After 90 days, your questions and mistakes will count against you. Don't make your boss wonder why he hired you in the first place.

10
BY
ENHANCING QUALITY

"Efficiency is doing things right;
effectiveness is doing the right things."
- Peter Drucker

How do you maintain quality results? Quality is the result of effectiveness, efficiency, and consistency.

What's Effectiveness?

This refers to the output produced from your business systems.

Effectiveness means successfully producing
a desired or intended result.

Effectiveness is future-oriented and involves achieving goals, anticipating change, and striving for innovation.

Effectiveness First, then Efficiency!

What's Efficiency?

Once you're effective, look for ways to become more efficient. This is done by finding ways to make your products and services better (faster, easier, lighter, smaller, more innovative, safer, and more secure)?

Efficiency means taking something that's
working well and making it better.

Your job is to make things better than you found them. Establish a reputation as the one who gets things done and is effective, efficient, and consistently produces excellent results. Efficiency focuses on the present and involves process improvement.

What's Consistency?

Consistency is critical to achieving success over time. For example, would you buy a car from a company that only produced a quality product, only one out of one hundred cars?

Consistency means maintaining a standard or repeating a task with minimal variation.

What happens to inconsistent NFL Football Coaches near the end of the season? They get fired! It's not personal; it's business! Consistency is fundamental to excellence, even if the output is consistently bad. You can improve any system if it's consistent in its output.

Quality Results =

Effectiveness + Efficiency + Consistency.

11
BY CREATING A
MISSION AND VISION STATEMENT

"Simplicity is the ultimate sophistication."
- Leonardo DaVinci

Do you know how to create a *Mission and a Vision Statement?*

What's a Mission Statement?

The best Mission Statement is a formal summary that explains what you do, how you do it, and why. It should provide a clearly stated purpose for your business and is designed for those you serve with your products or services.

What's a Vision Statement?

The best Vision Statement should shape your *Serving Philosophy* and culture and help guide you in the future. It should provide a clear goal to inspire those who produce your products or services.

What's the difference between a Mission and a Vision Statement?

According to Business Dictionary, a mission statement is

"a written declaration of an organization's core purpose and a focus that normally remains unchanged over time."

They also define a vision statement as *"an aspirational description of what an organization would like to achieve or accomplish in the mid-term or long-term future. It's intended to serve as a clear guide for choosing current and future courses of action."*

- A <u>Mission Statement</u> defines your purpose – something you want to accomplish and is created for your customers.

- A <u>Vision Statement</u> defines what you want to become in the future and is created to inspire your team members.

Here are a few examples of mission and vision statements from well-known corporations.

Make-A-Wish:

- <u>Mission</u>: To grant the wishes of children with life-threatening medical conditions to enrich the human experience with hope, strength, and joy.

- <u>Vision</u>: We are dedicated to making every eligible child's wish come true.

Goodwill:

- <u>Mission</u>: To enhance individuals and families' dignity and quality of life by strengthening communities, eliminating barriers to opportunity, and helping people in need reach their full potential through learning and the power of work.

- <u>Vision</u>: Every person has the opportunity to achieve their fullest potential and participate in and contribute to all aspects of life.

A Vision Statement inspires members to act. It's the driving force of your business and keeps your company focused on accomplishing something greater than themselves over the long term.

12
BY ALIGNING
FOCUS AND PRIORITIES

"Don't dwell on what went wrong. Instead, focus on what to do next.
Spend your energies on moving forward toward finding the answer."
- Denis Waitley

Do you know how to enhance your focus and priorities? Effective people ensure their focus and priorities are clear, well communicated, and are aligned with their boss's focus and priorities.

Before we talk about focus and priority, let's first answer this question.

What are the two most important things to every boss?

When I first started out in the **US Military**, I learned that success was a function of doing two things well:

Accomplishing the Mission and caring for Soldiers!

After I left the **US Military** and became an Executive Coach, I quickly found that effectiveness was a function of doing these two things well:

- *Productivity* means *"consistently producing excellent results."*

- *Sustainability* means *"adding value to all those who helped produce those results."*

By combining the two, here are the most important things you must do in business to become more effective:

Consistently produce excellent results and add value to
all those who helped you produce those results.

Now that you know the two most important things, let's examine how effective people determine their Focus and Priorities. First, focus and Priority must be directly linked to achieving your boss's goals. Often there's confusion as to the real meaning of Focus and Priority, but effective people aren't confused.

Effective people know that their effectiveness is about consistently producing excellent results linked to their boss's goals and adding value to those who helped them achieve their results. But how do they do that?

By knowing your Focus

Effective people focus their <u>time</u> and <u>energy</u> on completing one task or project at a time by:

- **Finding and Fixing** anything (Problems, Threats, Weaknesses) could slow or stop the achievement of their objective.

- **Discovering and Exploiting** anything (Opportunities, Strengths) that could enhance their goals by creating new and innovative ways to consistently produce excellent results that contribute to *Positive Cash Flow.*

- **Adding value to their team members** by applying and sharing what they've learned to help them become more effective and successful.

By knowing your Priorities

Effective people carefully <u>select the sequence</u> in which tasks and projects are completed by focusing on the work that has the greatest return by:

- **Providing Direction and Guidance** (the WHO, WHEN, and WHERE) to complete what needs to be done by approving goals, prioritizing tasks and projects, delegating authority, maintaining performance standards, resolving problems, planning, organizing, communicating, and operating. This allows team members the freedom to proactively take the initiative to modify plans and instructions to adapt to changing situations.

- **Providing a Common Purpose** (the WHY) that all members can support gives them a *Reason to Act.*

- **Adding value to their team members** by treating them with respect and kindness, supporting them in accomplishing their goals, facilitating collaborative problem-solving, protecting their *Health and Welfare,* and creating more effective team members for the future.

Note: Ensure your goals support your boss's goals.

13
BY IDENTIFYING
PRIORITY ACTIVITIES

"Do the hard jobs first.
The easy jobs will take care of themselves."
- Dale Carnegie

Do you know how to identify your priority activities?

A Priority Activity is the most important and least urgent activities that are only done "by choice" (like Planning and Training) and not being forced on you.

What's the Pareto Principle (The 80/20 Rule)?

A common "rule of thumb" in business is that 80% of your sales come from 20% of your clients, and 80% of your outcomes come from 20% of your inputs.

Other examples include:

- 20% of your activities produce 80% of your financial rewards.
- 20% of team members are responsible for 80% of a company's output.
- 20% of customers are responsible for 80% of the revenues.

In a business sense, using the *80/20 Rule* is crucial for maximizing performance. Effective people know which 20% of their activities will take them along the path to success faster and farther than others. They focus on completing those priority activities until finished.

Here are some suggestions:

- Find the products or services that generate the most income (20%) and drop marginal benefit (80%).
- Spend your time on the parts of your business unit that you can improve significantly by using your core skills and delegate all other tasks that are not your best skills (20%) to others.
- Work hardest on things that work hardest for you.

- Reward the best team members well; cull the worst.

- Drop your worst clients and focus on upselling and improving service with your best clients.

Use your team to help you identify your least urgent priority activities, such as training, preventive maintenance, relationship building, long-range planning, continuous improvement, organizing, developing members, prioritizing, and making things better.

How can you use a Power Hour?

Your *Power Hour* could be the 1st hour of the day. During this time, avoid all distractions. For example, don't process emails or voice mail messages, or you'll be working on someone else's priorities. Focus 100 % of your attention on your *Priority Activities* (what's most important but not urgent). What really matters?

14
BY UNDERSTANDING
BUSINESS SYSTEMS

Do you know all the internal Business Systems in your company?

Here you'll learn how they're created, maintained, and assessed, how to build quality into a system, the components of a *Business Operating System* (BOS), and how to assess and enhance your *Business Model.*

This is why effective people,

Serve members and manage everything else via systems.

A system can be a model, process, procedure, protocol, technique, pre-printed form, checklist, diagram, standard, or method. A system normally has five basic components: Requirement, Input, Process, Output, and Feedback.

Simple Systems Model

```
┌──────────┐    ┌──────────┐    ┌──────────┐
│  Input   │ ➡  │ Process  │ ➡  │  Output  │
└──────────┘    └──────────┘    └──────────┘
```

Feedback Loop

A system starts with a Requirement that directly links to achieving goals. The Requirement tells you the Output and answers the who, what, when, where (Direction), and why (Purpose). Working in reverse, the Output normally includes an assessment to ensure it meets the Requirement.

The system starts with a Requirement that directly links to achieving a goal. Once you know the Requirement (or Output), assess the Process needed to create the required Output. The Process includes execution, procedures, operations, activities, and transformation. After you've assessed the Process, assess the Input in terms of what is needed to produce the Output.

The Input normally includes planning, preparing, people, schedule, resources, budget, and raw materials. Now, assess to ensure your Input flows smoothly through the Process and assess the Output to see if it meets the Requirement of your #1 customer.

Next is your Feedback Loop, which provides information back to the Input and the Process concerning whether the Output satisfied the Requirement. If not, make the needed adjustments to either the Input or Process to meet the Requirement.

Breaking your system down into smaller subsystems will help you measure and assess the Output of each subsystem with the intent of making the entire system better able to satisfy the Requirement.

Where things get complicated is when a system is composed of several smaller subsystems

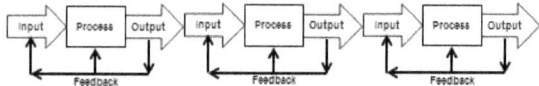

How do you assess a system?

Every business is a system comprised of numerous subsystems. How does your system interact with the other systems in your organization?

Here are the most important questions to ask about your systems:

- What're the systems and subsystems in my unit?

- What's the Output of every subsystem?

- How's this Output measured, and who's responsible for each system and subsystem?

- How does this person get trained, and what happens if he's gone?

- Is he the only person who knows how the system works?

- How do we reinforce or correct system flaws?

- What assessment system do we have to prevent and correct problems (Chapter 6)?

How do you maintain a system?

In most cases, you'll be responsible for maintaining the current systems rather than creating requirements or new systems. However, this doesn't stop you from making suggestions to make things better.

Who's your #1 customer or who uses your output?

In most cases, the Output of your unit will rarely go directly to the customer (end-user). It may go to another person or unit within your organization. If so, ask them, *"Are you completely satisfied with what we provide (our Output), and what can we do to make it better?"*

Many systems fail to achieve success because the boss didn't complete the Requirement first. Some bosses try to create the Requirement as they're building the Process and Input. *Big mistake!* Later, they had to go back and *undo* or *redo* specific actions because the Requirements were not correctly identified and approved before beginning work. The writing of the Requirements document must be created along with the client, customer, and end-users before action is taken.

Unless you receive *Buy-in* (a commitment, agreement, confirmation, or consensus) from the end-user of your unit's Output, you're setting yourself up for failure. *Buy-in* means that the end-user agrees that your system's Output meets their Requirements.

How do you create or change a system?

From the worst disasters, there are lessons learned to make things better. Why do you think we have organizations like the *National Transportation Safety Board (NTSB)?* After every airplane crash, the NTSB attempts to uncover what happened and what can be done to prevent it from happening again. Whenever something goes wrong, ask, "What happened and what system can prevent this from happening again?"

Now, create the systems needed to fix the problem. Are you and your unit *self-correcting* (Appendix G)? How can you take what you've learned and improve your system? By asking better HOW questions, you get to the heart of the problem. The goal here is to find out what was learned. Then, produce or modify systems that, if implemented, will change the course of future events.

Don't forget to celebrate what went right. Then, put in place the fixes that will create a better system. Create systems that measure your output, financial situation, customer attitudes, industry activity, and market trends to determine your relative position within your industry. Then, plot a course from where you are to where you want to be. What systems are in place to give you this information?

How do you build quality into your systems?

What's quality, and why should you be concerned? Quality relates to the output from your business unit or system, which directly results from the quality of the output from your internal subsystems.

Quality Results = Effectiveness + Efficiency + Consistency.

The three most important things to understand before building quality into your unit are your current output, the process that created it, and how it is measured.

How do you find the Delta?

The *Delta* is the difference between your *desired* and your *actual* end-state. Identify the *Delta* and create system enhancements to close the gap. Ask the team to come up with the solutions without telling them how to do it. What's the *standard* for the Output produced by your unit, how's it measured, where did it come from, and can this *standard* be improved (raising the bar)? If so, what's the cost?

Why should you document your system's processes?

Documenting means recording a process so someone else can continue the process in your absence.

The document should include all the steps from start to finish, along with any supporting pictures, diagrams, flowcharts, usernames and passwords, keys, and URLs needed to allow the reader to make the process work. The person responsible for the process should include this documentation in their Playbook (Chapter 16).

Effective people make every effort to document each process within their business unit to make the changes easier and quicker, provide insurance against absenteeism, and contribute to the *Cross-Training* (a technique of training each member how to perform the duties of two other members to minimize the effects of absenteeism) of their team members.

What are the components of a Business Operating System?

A Business Operating System (BOS) is the combination of subsystems needed to achieve the goals of an organization.

Effective people ensure each BOS has a designated *Person-In-Charge* (PIC) responsible for each subsystem and includes:

- Executive Leadership: Quality Management Program, review processes.
- Human Resources: Hiring, training, evaluations.
- Health, Safety, and Environment: Safeguard people and facilities.
- Information Technology: Communications, access to information
- Finance: Accounting processes.
- Purchasing: Sourcing, procurement, and supplier development
- Engineering: Common product and process development.
- Manufacturing: Common practices in each manufacturing facility.
- Sales: Trained team focused on new customer acquisition.
- Marketing:
  - ✓ Product – Identify what product you're focusing on.
  - ✓ Price – Identify your price and whether it's competitive.
  - ✓ Promotion – How will the product or service be promoted?
  - ✓ Place – Where will you target sales? Where will you manufacture the product?
  - ✓ Processes – Manufacturing, marketing, sales, and fulfillment.
  - ✓ People – Who's involved? What are their roles?

Do you have all these *Business Operating Systems*?

How do you assess your Business Model?

You already know the Project Model: Planning, Preparing, Executing, and Assessing.

A Business Model defines the process of how a company makes a profit.

Here are the most important questions to ask when creating your Business Model:

- What are the core aspects of your business, including purpose, offerings, strategies, infrastructure, organizational structures, trading practices, and operational processes and policies?

- How does your business create value, deliver that value, and "capture the value" provided?

- How does your business entice customers to "pay for value" and convert those payments into "profit"?

Does your *business model* address the above question, especially the *"capture the value," "pay for value,"* and the *"profit"* component?

Does your *business model* consistently provide *Positive Cash Flow*? If not, why are you in business?

15

BY SCALING THE BUSINESS

"Strive for continuous improvement, instead of perfection."
- Kim Collins

How can you scale your business?

Scaling means setting the stage to enable and support future growth.

Scalability is about capacity and capability. If growth is causing your company to stumble because orders are going unfulfilled or delayed due to insufficient staff, miscommunication, not enough manufacturing or delivery capacity, you need to scale your business.

Scaling is about increasing revenue at a rapid rate while increasing your efficiency at an incremental rate.

As you build your business, think about how to scale it, not just increase revenue. If you continue increasing revenue by adding more customers without a corresponding investment to increase efficiency, your growth will stagnate because you won't keep up with the demand.

Efficiency means adding *technology, people, infrastructure, and systems* to streamline and strengthen your ability to better satisfy customers, reduce cost, increase efficiency and productivity, and become more responsive.

How do you scale a business?

To scale your business, create a *Plan of Action* that focuses on increasing your company's efficiency and acquiring new business. The best plan to scale your business starts with a detailed sales growth forecast, broken down by the number of new customers, orders, and revenue you want to generate. Also, do an expense forecast based on adding *technology, people, infrastructure, and systems* to handle those new sales orders.

Start by anticipating what you need to increase sales. Then assume your orders doubled or tripled overnight. Do you have the *technology, people, infrastructure, and systems* to handle those new orders?

What Technology is needed?

Do you have the systems to:

- Generate more sales (sales structure)?
- Generate the desired number of leads (sufficient lead flow)?
- Track and manage leads (Marketing systems)?
- Follow up and close leads (Enough sales representatives)?
- Manage sales orders?
- Follow up to ensure invoices are collected timely (billing system and receivables)?
- Create reports to measure and manage results?

You can gain huge economies of scale, leverage, and more throughput, with less labor if you invest wisely in technology.

What People are needed?

Build a network of partners, such as service providers, sales channel partners, suppliers, and customers. Do you have enough customer service staff? To find qualified help quickly, use **Zip Recruiter.com**. Sometimes the best solution is to outsource or look to partners rather than hire internally. Find a reliable partner to outsource, and position your business to scale better, faster, and cheaper.

What Infrastructure is needed?

Infrastructure means the basic structure of a company, including buildings, equipment, vehicles, furniture, machinery, tools, parking, communication, sewage, water, and electric systems needed to create your product or offer your service.

What Systems and Processes are needed?

Systems integration is the essential building block of every company. Simply stated, a business system takes care of your future. Look for a good Customer Relationship Management (CRM) system to manage your marketing, sales, inventory, manufacturing, accounting, HR, shipping, and other technology systems. Systems are the foundation for establishing a simple, flexible, scalable, and manageable operation. The core of your IT environment typically includes hardware like servers, computers, printers, telephony equipment, storage, networking, and end-user devices.

16
BY CREATING A
PLAYBOOK

"Finding good players is easy.
Getting them to play as a team is another story."
- Casey Stengel

Do you know how to create a *Playbook* for each team member?

A Playbook is a collection of the most important tactics, techniques, and tools needed by a member to perform their job.

A Playbook should include all company processes, policies, and standard operating procedures needed to execute faster, smoother, and easier than your competition, especially when it comes to *scaling.*

Every team member should have a *Playbook* consisting of either a three-ring binder or its digital equivalent.

As a minimum, each *Playbook* should contain:

- Their duties, responsibilities, expectations, constraints, authority, projects, and standards.
- Organizational charts and diagrams and SOPs.
- Rules of Conduct and Training Actions.
- A listing of all assignments you've completed and are working on.
- Formats for standard documents, like a Decision Paper.
- Usernames, passwords, phone numbers, combinations, and URLs.
- Operating instructions for all his systems.
- All recurring events, like weekly, monthly, quarterly, and annual.
- A copy of their boss's *Serving Philosophy.*
- A listing of any tools or equipment for which you're responsible.
- A list of expectations for meetings and internal communication.

Without having some form of *Playbook* for each team member, where do you want them to go to find this information? It should be used (or exchanged) when a new member transitions in or out of your unit. *Playbooks* will make your in-processing and transitioning process easier. Every company needs a *Playbook* to scale successfully (Chapter 16).

What are the Advantages of a Playbook?

A *Playbook* helps:

- Teams stay aligned, and members stay accountable.
- The company scale successfully.
- Anyone on the team can fill any position.
- Keep the business running smoothly.
- Explain how the business does what it does, down to each role and responsibility.

Playbooks also permit team members to cross-train to help offset the effects of absenteeism and turnover. Without a *Playbook*, this leaves members guessing the best, safest, or most efficient way to do something. If your members have to guess what to do, this will cost you time and money in the long run.

What are the steps to create a Playbook?

The most important steps to create a *Playbook are:*

Step 1. List: Ask each team member to list every important task for which they're responsible.

Step 2. Consolidate: Consolidate the tasks from each team member to ensure there are no duplications of duties and responsibilities.

Step 3. Alignment: How do these tasks relate to their boss's goals?

Step 4. Objective: What's the objective for each task. Who else is involved, what, when, where, and why?

Step 5. Method: Ask each member to outline how each task should be performed with pictures, diagrams, and examples.

Step 6. Risk: What's the probability and impact of what you could lose and what could *reasonably-go-wrong*?

Step 7. Timetable: When do you start, and how long will it take?

Step 8. Resources: What will you need?

Step 9. Unresolved Issues: Capture and eliminate any *Unresolved Issues* that could slow or stop your progress (Chapter 25).

Step 10. Update: Every quarter, update all *Playbooks* by looking for opportunities to improve how you do things. As you find better practices, you'll need to update the *Playbook*.

Playbooks ensure that each team member is empowered to do their best work moving forward. Every company needs *Playbooks* to scale their business successfully (Chapter 16).

17
BY MAXIMIZING THE
TIME AVAILABLE

"If you love life, don't waste time, for time is what life is made up of."
– Bruce Lee

Have you ever wished you could just *stop-the-train* for a little while, just long enough to get caught up or just finish something? We all have. Effective people know that no one can manage time. It's the same as trying to manage the weather.

Here are several suggested ways to make that happen.

By eliminating Time Wasters.

From *The Time Trap*, by **R. Alex Mackenzie.**

- Telephone interruptions and visitors dropping in.

- Meetings are both scheduled and unscheduled.

- Crisis situations where no plans were possible or created.

- Lack of focus, priorities, and deadlines; indecision, procrastination, and fatigue.

- Cluttered desk and personal disorganization.

- Involved in routine details that should be delegated.

- Underestimated the amount of time required to get things done.

- Failure to set-up clear lines of authority and responsibility.

- Inadequate, inaccurate, or delayed information from others.

- Unclear instructions and the inability to say NO.

- Lack of standards and *Update Briefings* to track progress.

Additional Time Wasters: Negative emotions, last-minute changes, ignorance, laziness, apathy, and complacency.

By using these Time Saving Tips.

- Establish a quiet period to provide uninterrupted concentration.
- Consolidate outgoing calls and don't allow incoming calls.
- Ensure someone screens visitors and blocks interruptions.
- Identify time wasters and resolve them.
- Establish fixed hours for team members to visit.
- Have them state their purpose and the time needed.
- Visit their office so you can leave when you're done.
- Have members bring recommended solutions, not just problems.
- Conduct your meetings standing up.
- Make a habit of meeting monthly for lunch with each member.
- Have your assistant dial calls for you *(Please hold for Bob)*. But don't use this with your boss.

By owning the Day!

Here are the best questions to get more done in the same 8-hour day.

- Do your focus and priorities support your boss?
- How can you better organize and plan?
- Have can you identify and eliminate redundancies?
- Which processes (systems) need to be improved?
- Have you consolidated, simplified, or eliminated waste?
- Have you identified things that need to be standardized?
- Which duties should be *cross-trained (if someone gets sick)?
- Have you identified things that need to be streamlined?
- What's distracting your focus? What takes too much time?
- What training is needed for your team members?
- Have you found any **Economies of Scale?
- What else could be delegated?
- How do you avoid running out of needed supplies?

- Have you eliminated your time wasters?

- How can you use a ***Dashboard* or a *FAQ* site?

- How can you better anticipate opportunities and problems?

Cross-training: The process of training each team member to perform the duties of two other members.

**Economy of scale:* Reduction of per-unit costs through an increase in production volume.

***Dashboard* (Chapter 23) or *Frequently Asked Question* site.

By using Standard Formats.

Create standard formats for your members, like a Decision Paper, Position Paper, Memorandum for Record, Plan of Action, Contingency Plan, Mitigation Plan, Unresolved Issues List, Assignment Log, Change List, Timetable, Project Update Briefing, Authorization Matrix, and Decision Support Template.

By giving Team Members a Break.

This section is concerned with fairness and treating others with respect and kindness. These options are based on how much you trust your team members. This is a great way to show your trust in them.

- **Comp-Time:** This is time granted by a boss to a member who works past normal work hours or on the weekend. This lets the member either come in a few hours later or leave a few hours earlier the next day.

- **Flex-Time:** This time lets members set their schedule that best fits their personal life (child care and commuting), as long as they're present for scheduled meetings.

- **Telecommuting:** This lets members work from home and is advisable for those with a long commute. This could include a periodic visit to the office once a week or a few times a month.

If you're more concerned with productivity and getting things done, these options should be considered rather than counting heads or filling seats every day. If your members are happy and consistently producing excellent results, why would you care where or when they work? Sounds like a win-win to me!

This page is intentionally left blank.

18
BY IDENTIFYING AND EXPLOITING OPPORTUNITIES

"Problems are only opportunities in work clothes."
- Henry J. Kaiser

Do you know how to identify and exploit opportunities? Effective people know that opportunities abound. There are only two reasons you're not taking advantage of these opportunities; either you don't know what you're looking for or not looking in the right places.

Here's an example to get you thinking:

"Years ago, Stanley Steamer started as a company that just cleaned carpets. However, they had to find a new and innovative way to add services to what they were already doing because of competition. So today, they have expanded to cleaning any flooring (wood, vinyl, concrete). They also clean heating and air conditioning ducts, and who knows what else."

What are the most important questions to identify and exploit opportunities?

- Who and where are our competitors?
- What's our competition doing?
- How can we beat our competition?
- Who's watching our competition and what's he looking for?
- Does he have the resources needed?
- Who and how often does he report his findings?
- What systems do we have in place to identify opportunities?
- What signs or signals is our system looking for?
- Who's responsible for this system?
- Where is he looking, and what is he looking for?
- Does he have the resources needed?
- Who and how often does he report his findings?
- What's our *Unique Selling Proposition (USP)*?

- Why would someone buy from us and not the competition?

- What's our **Competitive Advantage*?

- Are there other services your team could provide to your current customers?

- Have our members participated in a *Brainstorming* session to address this problem?

- When was the last time a ***Customer Focus Group* was used?

- What other non-competing companies have access to our customers?

- Are there other companies that we could partner with to help you grow?

- Are there any government agencies that could use our product or service?

- Are there any religious organizations that could use our product or service?

- How can we leverage our existing relationships with our current customers?

Unique Selling Proposition: This is a marketing concept first proposed as a theory to explain a pattern in successful advertising campaigns of the early 1940s and states that such campaigns made unique propositions to customers that convinced them to switch brands.

**Competitive Advantage*: This is when an organization develops an attribute that allows it to outperform its competitors, like a special tax exemption.

***Customer Focus Group*: This involves a group of people randomly selected to candidly assess products and services for usability, cost, variety, and complaints.

If you aren't seriously looking for opportunities, guess what your competition is doing?

19
BY RESPONDING TO
CUSTOMER FEEDBACK

"By providing memorable social media customer service, companies not only create deeper connections with consumers, but they glean valuable insights on how to improve their products or services."
- Amy Jo Martin

Do you know how to collect, process, and respond to customer feedback?

Care enough to give your customers what they really want— rather than what they think they want.

How do you know if your customers are satisfied with what you're providing them? Their feedback is critical to your success.

Find out what customers really want and care enough to help them get it.

Feedback from your customers, if captured and acted on, will lead to your long-term success.

Who are your best customers?

Most people in the workforce don't deal directly with the end-user. Instead, they deal with other members, vendors, suppliers, or different departments within their company. Whoever they are, when was the last time you asked them what you could do to make a greater contribution?

Create ways to collect and process customer feedback

For example, luxury car companies have one designated person in each sales area that periodically calls all car owners to conduct a survey. The purpose of the survey is to gather information about customer satisfaction and to resolve problems immediately. Each survey is graded with the scores reported to Corporate Headquarters. These survey results determine end-of-year bonuses.

Create an "I can make it right" environment.

How many times have you been frustrated by customer service members who had no authority or resources to satisfy your problem or complaint? This has become the norm and the acceptable standard of service across the country.

Empower your team members with the resources to make it right for all customers.

This requires that they be trained, have the resources and the authority necessary to resolve customer problems (like *Enterprise Rent-A-Car*).

Stay connected to your customers.

Listening to your customers is vitally important to your success. You don't have to do everything they say. But, listening to them is in your best interest.

Here are the most important questions to ask your customers frequently:

- What was wasted, not used, or a waste of time?
- What was too hard (a hassle), too expensive, or what took too long?
- What do you really like? What did you dislike?
- What broke or didn't work properly?
- What was difficult to understand or use?
- What suggestions do you have to make things better?

Now develop a *Plan of Action* to address each answer. Finally, tell all *Key Players* if things change.

Here's what **Elon Musk** did when a *Tesla* customer complained on Twitter:

Customer: *"Can you guys program the car once in 'park' to move back the seat and raise the steering wheel? Steering wheel is wearing."*

Elon Musk: *"Good point. We will add that to all cars in one of the upcoming software releases."*

That's one way to use social media effectively. Who monitors your social media? To whom does he report? Unfortunately, many companies make excuses, shift blame or responsibility to another department, or some other form of stalling that usually results in the death of good ideas. What a waste!

Create "Raving Fans."

I'm a *Raving Fan* of two great restaurants locally. I'm a *Raving Fan* because of their Servers. What is a *Raving Fan*? As **Ken Blanchard** wrote in his book,

"A Raving Fan is a customer who is so devoted to your products and services that they wouldn't dream of taking their business elsewhere and will sing from the rooftops about just how good you are."

To create a *Raving Fan*, a Server must:

- Always be cheerful, respectful, and attentive
- Remember what we like to order and how we like it delivered
- Pay attention to the details and anticipate our needs
- Never let your drinks run out
- Hustle – and always make things right!

Oh, and did I mention that the food is great, the price is excellent, and the portions are generous. Incredible! And, in addition to leaving a nice tip, how else do I show that I'm a *Raving Fan*?

I dine there several times per month, tell all my friends who enjoy good food, give them the server's name, brag to the owner about their great servers. I also bring guests there to dine, and I submit a glowing review of them on *Trip Advisor.com*. Service, Service, Service will win the day every time!

Your goal is to convert current customers into Raving Fans to gain new customers through referrals!

Never violate the Laws of Customer Service.

The First Law of Customer Service says,

Always under-promise and over-deliver.

If you tell someone you'll deliver next Tuesday, you better deliver no later than Tuesday. And if you can deliver on Monday, you'll be the hero. Most often, however, the customer gets the call that it can't be delivered until Wednesday. Now you've lost credibility with your customer.

If you have any doubts as to when you can deliver, don't make the promise in the first place.

Call them back when you have a firm date. And, if the unthinkable happens, and you have to break the bad news to the customer, make whatever concessions you need to make (reduce the price or provide an upgrade) to lessen the disappointment. But, remember, it's a small world, and people talk. So, treat them the way you wish to be treated if you were the customer.

The Second Law of Customer Service says,

Never make excuses!

Customers hate excuses! They make you look weak and disorganized! If you're not certain you can deliver, don't make the promise in the first place. If things go wrong, figure out what went wrong, and fix it for good! Customers hate flaky people - people they can't trust to deliver what they promise.

The Third Law of Customer Service says,

Never run out of your most popular stuff.

Know your inventory and your schedule cold! Order replacements or resupply well before you expect to run out, especially when it's your most popular stuff.

20
BY CREATING A
BUSINESS PROPOSAL

"Either write something worth reading or do something worth writing."
- Benjamin Franklin.

Writing a Business Proposal is another form of writing to persuade. In this case, you're trying to persuade someone to do business with you. There are two kinds of business proposals: Solicited and Unsolicited.

By Creating a Solicited Business Proposal

Solicited proposals are created in response to a client's needs. They're a key step in the sales process. These proposals work well for government and independent contractors, small business owners, and those who do part-time work for websites like

Upwork, PeoplePerHour, Freelancer, Guru, Hubstaff Talent, ServiceScape, Outsourcely, TaskRabbit, and LinkedIn ProFinder.

Success Tip 1.
Always be selling the problems you solve, rather than the products or services you offer.

Thanks to **Don Miller** and his great team at *StoryBrand.com*, here are the most important steps to create a winning business proposal.

Step 1. My Problem.

For example, let's assume that I'm the client. I've just posted an online solicitation for someone to help me create a computer application that helps parents teach their children responsibility, even while on vacation.

There are three levels to my problem.

- **My External Problem.** I need someone to create a software application.

- **My Internal Problem.** I need someone who understands how frustrating it is to teach children responsibility, especially while on vacation.

- **My Philosophical Problem.** This is the most difficult task I face as a parent. Every parent needs a way to impart these values to their children before they become adults.

Your proposal should consistently agitate all three levels of my problem.

Remember, I don't care about you or your company until you've proven that you care about me and my problem.

Step 2. Your Solution.

What benefits will I experience after hiring you?

Always focus on how your solution will enhance my Happiness, Success, or Freedom.

Explain how you can eliminate my problem or satisfy my need by stressing your benefits, not the features.

> **Success Tip 2.**
> *Always be selling the problems you solve, rather than the products or services you offer.*

Step 3. Your Plan.

What are the three simple steps needed for me to do business with you? Each step of your plan should be accompanied by a brief statement that describes the benefit to me. For example, if step one in your plan is to *"Schedule a Call,"* the statement should describe what benefits I'll experience by taking this step. What are the three steps I must take to do business with you? Keep it simple.

Step 4. The Price.

Always frame your price as an investment in me and my family. Also, explain the cost of not hiring you. Offer payment options like split payments, financing, or other discounts or incentives. Also, to create a sense of urgency, create a deadline by stating that your pricing expires in 14 days.

Step 5. The Guide.

This is your opportunity to tell your story to establish your authority and empathy.

- **Authority** is your ability to explain how you've already helped others with a similar need. By doing so, you're creating trust and credibility. This is done through success stories, social proof, and customer testimonials.

- **Empathy** is your ability to convince me that you understand how I feel by living with my problem. For example, write things like, "We care about you..." or "We know how frustrating this must be..."

Step 6. Explain your Offer.

Explain how your offer helps me overcome my problem and achieve my goal. Always focus on how your solution will enhance my:

Happiness, Success, or Freedom.

Success Tip 3.
Always be selling the problems you solve, rather than the products or services you offer.

Hopefully, by now, you're starting to figure out that this is the most important guiding principle for all successful sales and marketing on the planet today. If you lose focus and wander away from this principle, which should be your core message, and start bragging about how great your company is, you've lost me as a potential client forever. Period! End of story!

Step 7. The Call to Action.

This is where I should find a "Call Now" with your phone number. Then, begin your closing by using language like, "We want your business. Just choose your options, and "Call Now." Or "Here's how to get started right now. Accept this proposal, and let's do this together. Call Now!"

Step 8. Describe what success feels like.

Paint a word-picture of what my life will be like after I hire you. Be clear and specific by focusing on how your solution will enhance my,

Happiness, Success, or Freedom.

Step 9. Second Call to Action!

Include another "Call Now" and include it several times!

Step 10. A PS Section.

Your PS could include a limited-time offer or a bonus, or it could focus on what I'll lose by not doing business with you.

Here's the *bottom-line* on Proposals:

> *Don't be afraid to ask for the sale unless you*
> *don't believe in what you're selling!*

It shows confidence in your ability to overcome my problem and helps position you as my guide.

> *Oh, by the way, for those parents who're looking for an application to help you teach responsibility to your children even while on vacation, check out **busy kid.com.***

By Creating an Unsolicited Business Proposal

Writing an unsolicited business proposal is different and, in some ways, more challenging. When writing unsolicited proposals, you have no clue what problems a prospective client is facing.

This proposal has the same format as the solicited proposal except for Step 1, *The Problem.* Since this is an unsolicited proposal, you're guessing what their problems might be. However, based on the products or services you provide, you should have a pretty good idea of what you can do for a new client.

Why did they hire you? What problems have you already resolved for your clients? Focus on those problems. Highlight the negative feelings your clients felt before they hired you. What was important to them? What were their pain points? Now, just follow the same steps from the solicited proposal.

Many people use a sales brochure or a sales landing page for this purpose. They also create a pdf lead generator and add it to their website. What you may not have noticed, you just learned how to write a sales letter, a .pdf lead generator, a sales brochure, a web landing page, and the script for a sales presentation. **You're welcome!**

21
BY
TAKING-CHARGE

When in doubt, mumble; when in trouble,
delegate; when in charge, ponder.
- James H. Boren

This chapter assumes that you've been assigned a project by your boss, and you're in the process of *taking-charge* as the Project Manager (PM).

Important Terms and Concepts

Backbriefing:

A briefing given by the Project Manager (PM) to his boss BEFORE starting a project, explaining how the PM intends to accomplish the boss's objective.

Being in-charge:

This means that you're the boss of a project (an assignment that requires the effort of others) assigned by your boss. Sometimes, your boss will make you the coordinator for a project. It could also be called the lead, point person, or facilitator. These are all ways of saying that you're *in-charge* with limitations.

When in-charge, take-charge!

Only your boss can tell you the extent of those limitations. If in doubt, ask! Make no assumptions. Do you have the authority to make decisions, task others, assign work, hire, fire, spend money, and set priorities? This is why you should always conduct a *Backbriefing* with your boss.

Boss:

The person you report to for your work assignments and pays you for your products and services.

Briefback:

A question and answer meeting called by the PM to ensure all participants understand the Plan of Action, their duties and responsibilities, consequences and effects, unresolved issues, and what to do when things go wrong.

Flexibility to Respond:

As the PM, you represent your boss in everything you do to ensure the project's success. However, you must retain your *Flexibility to Respond* because plans and projects rarely unfold as expected.

> **Flexibility to Respond is your Freedom of Action**
> **to check on your project, resolve problems, and remain**
> **responsive to your members and your boss.**

This means always staying in contact with all participants and your boss, being free to roam and reposition your members, equipment, or supplies to where they're most needed. That means that you must delegate any problems or obstacles to another team member or Key Play so that you don't get diverted with ancillary issues causing you to take your eye off the big picture. Once you get bogged down as a doer, you're no longer the PM.

Effective PMs are in-motion checking and encouraging!

Key Player:

Anyone who must perform a task for your project to succeed and doesn't report to you (like a vendor, supplier, or a member of a different department).

Project:

Any assignment that requires the effort of others to achieve the objective and includes achieving goals, resolving problems, and conducting activities or events.

Project Manager:

The person assigned by the boss to conduct a project: the *person-in-charge*.

Tasking Authority:

Your ability to assign work to another member. For example, you only have *tasking authority* over your direct reports, which are those members who report to you for their work assignments. If they don't work for you, you have no *tasking authority*. However, your boss and his boss have *tasking authority* over many more members that can be assigned to you temporally to complete your project.

Team Member:

This includes anyone who normally reports to you for their work assignments, your Direct Reports.

By knowing what a Project Manager does

When In-Charge, Take-Charge!

What are the most important things a PM should do?

- Always protect your *Flexibility to Respond.*

- Step up and take responsibility and accountability for a project from start to finish (Appendix F).

- Ask questions, listen to concerns, pay attention, and delegate authority, but never responsibility.

- Build consensus with the team.

- Facilitate problem-solving and collaboration.

- Be willing to change the plan when needed, demonstrate flexibility, and adapt to changing conditions.

- When things go wrong, you own the mistakes. When things go well, you share the success.

- Be proactive and responsive by checking and making things happen!

- Provide a Backbriefing to your boss to ensure you understand his expectations.

What should a PM NOT do?

As the PM, you should NOT:

- Become engaged in physically helping a team member because it limits your *Flexibility to Respond* elsewhere.

- Attempt to resolve problems or unresolved issues. Delegate it to a team member.

Here's a Great Story

One day, John (the boss) visited a work site to check on a sub-project conducted by one of his Direct Reports (Bob). John asked Bob how things were going. Bob had two job sites as part of his sub-project.

John then visited Bob's second job site and saw that the members there were doing nothing. Bob's members tried to call Bob but got no answer. John tried to call Bob but got no response. Frustrated, John drove back to the first site and asked Bob why he wasn't answering his phone. Bob said his phone was in his truck.

John then pulled Bob aside for some on-the-job correcting and said, "Bob, I need you to have your phone with you at all times. Also, I just came from your second site and found that your team had no idea what they were supposed to do. I need you to get over there to straighten things out. Also, you need to check both your sites first thing every morning to ensure they get started the right way.

Bob lost his *Flexibility to Respond* because he left his phone in his truck, and no one could contact him.

Are you a Micro-Manager?

Well, let's see. The opposite of effective delegation is micromanagement.

Micromanagement is a management style whereby the boss closely observes and controls the work of a Direct Report.

Micromanagement also includes the suppression of constructive criticism that could otherwise lead to internal reform and job turnover. In micromanagement, the boss not only tells the Direct Report WHAT to do but dictates HOW to do it.

A frequent cause of micromanagement comes from the boss's doubt whether the Direct Report is competent enough to complete the project. Effective delegation requires a well-defined objective, a clear vision of the constraints and dependencies, and effective oversight.

So, are you a micro-manager? Do you trust your Direct Reports? Would they agree? Any room for improvement?

22

BY CONDUCTING A
BACKBRIEFING

"Progress always involves risks. You can't steal
second base and keep your foot on first."
- Frederick B. Wilcox

This chapter assumes that your boss assigned you as the Project Manager (PM) for an upcoming project. One way to ensure no unmet expectations and misunderstandings between you and your boss before your next project is to conduct a Backbriefing.

A Backbriefing is a briefing given by the Project Manager to his boss BEFORE starting a project, explaining how the PM intends to accomplish the boss's objective.

As far as your boss is concerned, if he assigned you to be the *person-in-charge* of an assignment - the assignment belongs to you – and you're the Project Manager.

Backbriefings are a good way to achieve a "meeting of the minds" before work begins. They enhance mutual understanding and trust by exchanging questions and answers to ensure no unmet expectations or hidden surprises later. They benefit all parties by reducing misunderstandings and the need for rework. They also enhance your credibility, thus relieving the need for micromanagement.

When should a Backbriefing be conducted?

In business, there are two types of projects.

- **Expected Projects** are projects already part of your job description, like an annual trade show. For expected projects, provide a Backbriefing at least 90 days before the project.

- **Requested Projects** are newly assigned projects and should receive a Backbriefing a week after receiving the assignment.

Here are the most important steps to conduct a good Backbriefing:

Step 1. Conduct an Initial Site Inspection.

Visit the site to see if it meets the requirements. If you're asked to select the best site, visit several sites and present the best to your boss. Gather sufficient information (like photos, dimensions, and sketch maps) to help you create your Draft Plan of Action (Appendix A) and prepare for your Backbriefing (Chapter 22). The most important issues when picking the best site are location, availability, accessibility, and cost.

Step 2. Create your Draft Plan of Action.

Use the Plan of Action Checklist in (Appendix A) to create your draft.

Step 3. Identify and eliminate all Unresolved Issues.

An Unresolved Issue is any question, unknown, concern, shortfall, obstacle, or problem that could slow or stop your progress (Chapter 25).

Step 4. Anticipate the Consequences and Effects.

List any Unintended Consequences and Second and Third-Order Effects (Chapter 26). Work hard to find anyone who has done this or a similar work before. What problems, consequences, and effects did they have?

Step 5. Conduct a Risk Assessment.

Assess the risk of anything that could slow or stop your project or cause physical harm, security failures, and financial loss and how they can be mitigated (Chapter 32).

Step 6. Brief your boss using the Plan of Action Checklist (Appendix A).

- You're not expected to have all the answers, but you're expected to have all the questions. So, as a minimum, obtain answers to these questions:

- What's the desired end-result or objective?

- How will success be measured?

- What are all the most important tasks that must be completed?

- Who's responsible for each major task?

- What's your authority to make decisions and spend money?

Then, set the schedule for periodic Project Updates (Chapter 23). Capture any new Unresolved Issues or questions your boss asked that you couldn't answer. If the boss doesn't want a Backbriefing, send him your draft POA and get his approval.

Step 7. Create a Memorandum of Record.

Finally, create a memo documenting what happened during the Backbriefing and any questions you couldn't answer. Ensure your boss and all Key Players get a copy. If you fail to conduct a Backbriefing with your boss before your next project, do so at your peril.

You've been WARNED!

By conducting a Briefback

After your team members have received your plan, ask them if they have any questions.

A Briefback is a synchronization meeting conducted by the PM with all team members present to ensure they all understand their duties, responsibilities, expectations, and what to do in case something goes wrong.

Briefbacks are critical because the process of giving instructions always leaves room for misunderstandings. They also reduce waste by preventing rework and are an effective tool to manage ambiguity.

As the PM, Briefbacks help you enhance your ability to give clearer instructions. Ask them to tell you the role they play. You can also ask them specific questions about the plan to confirm their understanding. This also allows them to ask you questions.

Address all the *"What ifs"* to help identify all the risks, expectations, assumptions, unintended consequences, 2d and 3d-order effects, unresolved issues, and the contingency plans needed.

Assume nothing! Whenever you assume anything, you risk making an 'ass' out of 'u' and 'me.' So, be careful! The simple fact is that if you don't do what your boss wanted, it doesn't matter if your instructions, either oral and written, were clear or not: you'll still be starting over.

Look, here's the bottom-line on good communications.

Good communication isn't about you - it's about them.

Do they understand what you want to be done? And how do you know for sure? You won't know unless you ask! And whose responsible and accountable if they don't understand and the project goes bad? Get a clue!

If you use this simple technique, you'll never have to say, *"I didn't know they didn't know."*

23

BY CONDUCTING A
PROJECT UPDATE

*"It takes half your life before you discover
life is a do-it-yourself project."*
- Napoleon Hill

How do you ensure your boss knows the current status of your projects?

**A Project Update is a summary of a project provided to the boss
and all Key Players as to the current status of a project.**

Your boss may have some changes or modifications to the original *Plan of
Action*. These last-minute changes are usually the things that complicate
any project. So, prepare for these changes, document them carefully, and
communicate them to all Key Players. There are two ways to provide a
Project Update, either by a Briefing or a Dashboard.

By conducting a Project Update Briefing

Here are the most important steps.

Step 1: Overall assessment.

When reporting the summary, give the *bottom-line*, *up-front*. Then,
justify your assessment. How's the assignment doing in relation to the
scope, schedule, money, and people from the original POA?

- **Positive assessments:** On-schedule, within budget, looking
  good, progressing nicely.

- **Negative assessments:** Behind schedule, in trouble, over-
  budget, or has major problems.

Step 2: Unresolved Issues.

Present any question, unknown, concern, shortfall, obstacle, or problem
that could slow or stop your progress (Chapter 25). If new problems are
introduced, the boss will expect you to present options to resolve these
problems and recommend which option is best. Your boss will also
expect you to have already presented the problem to all Key Players for
their concurrence or non-concurrence with comments (Chapter 27).

Step 3: Changes.

Present any new changes since your last briefing.

Step 4: Close.

Close by summarizing and restating any assignments made during the briefing or any Follow-through action (Chapter 30). Confirm the date and time of the next update. Prepare a Memorandum for Record (MFR) to document what happened during the meeting.

By creating a Project Update Dashboard

The most popular type of business dashboard is the Google Analytics Dashboards, used on 55% of all websites, which shows the activity on a website, like visits, entry pages, bounce rate, and traffic sources.

A Dashboard is a graphic or picture providing at-a-glance views or "snap-shots" of Key Performance Indicators (KPIs) relevant to a project's objective or a business process.

It's posted where all Key Players can access it (like a shared-drive so all can check progress, 24/7).

Here's an example of a Dashboard.

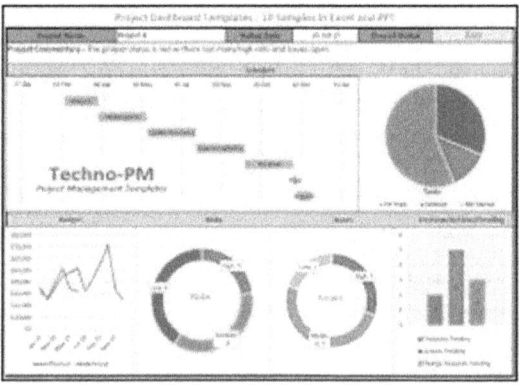

If done manually, ensure you update it every week or as changes occur. Email any changes to all concerned. Since a Dashboard is intended to provide the same material as a Project Update Briefing, design it to quickly give the same important information. You can also add links to other documents, like Frequently Asked Questions (FAQ).

24

BY CONDUCTING
INTERNAL MEETINGS

Murphy's Law on Meetings:
A meeting is an event at which the minutes
are kept, and the hours are lost.

Have you ever been to a meeting that was a waste of time, and you just wanted to leave? Was it your meeting? Today, many face-to-face, sit-down meetings are often unproductive, especially when considering all the advanced communication technology available. However, meetings can be productive and meaningful, and here are a few suggestions:

1. Simplify your Agenda.

Most meetings I've attended failed to get to the heart of the problems needing attention. Here are the most important components:

- **Present:** What are you currently working on, and when do you expect to finish?

- **Future:** What are you planning to accomplish before our next meeting?

- **Unresolved Issues:** Do you have any questions, unknowns, concerns, shortfalls, obstacles, or problems that could slow or stop your progress (Chapter 25)?

After starting the meeting, go around the room and ask everyone to comment on their three agenda items. You may even ask that everyone submit their three agenda items via email to you or the meeting facilitator the day before. This way, a copy of each person's response can be provided to all participants at the meeting.

2. Preside instead of conduct.

Ask someone else to conduct your meeting so that you can preside. Conducting a meeting is good training for your #2 person. It allows you to observe the body language, note who's not participating, and inject, clarifies, question, reinforce, or redirect, as needed.

3. Hold members accountable (Appendix G).

In a non-threatening way, *accountability* means asking:

- How are you progressing on your assignments?
- How do you intend to resolve your problems?
- Do you need more time or other resources?

If someone needs more time to complete an assignment, consider renegotiating a new deadline (Appendix E).

4. Don't get distracted.

The reason for not dealing with new, non-emergency, *Unresolved Issues* is to avoid being distracted and losing focus during your meeting. If a new *Unresolved Issue* is brought up, that's a non-emergency and can't be resolved quickly; you have several options.

- Assign someone to lead another meeting to resolve the issue. Assign all others that you feel need to be at that meeting.
- Assign the person who brought up the issue to write a *Decision Paper* (Appendix C).
- Assign the person who brought up the issue to come to see you with a recommended solution before the next meeting.

Most importantly, don't leave this issue without an assignment. Near the end of the meeting, review all assignments made during the meeting.

5. Consider setting these expectations.

- Meetings start and end on time and last no more than one hour.
- If you can't attend, send someone to discuss your agenda items.
- Bad language isn't permitted, and only one person speaks at a time.
- No throwing anyone *under-the-bus*, especially if not present.
- Do everything you can to support each other (Teamwork is critical).
- No distractions, no texting or communicating on any devices.
- I expect your 100% attention, involvement, and participation.
- I expect you to treat everyone with respect and kindness
- Come to participate, contribute, encourage, and help others.

25

BY ELIMINATING
UNRESOLVED ISSUES

*"There are two ways of spreading light: to be the candle
or the mirror that reflects it."*
- Edith Wharton

Do you know how to identify and eliminate any uncertainty that could stop
or slow your ability to consistently produce excellent results?

**An Unresolved Issue is any question, unknown,
concern, shortfall, obstacle, or problem that
could slow or stop your progress.**

Your mission is to hunt down and eliminate all the *Unresolved Issues*
associated with your work. If you don't, *Murphy's Law* will surely ruin
your day. Don't let this happen to you!

So, do yourself a favor. Identify and eliminate all your *Unresolved Issues*
early on to avoid the frustration, mistakes, and potential failure that could
result from not having *your-act-together.*

Here are the most important steps to eliminate all your *Unresolved Issues.*

Step 1. Identify all Issues.

To identify all your *Unresolved Issues*, seek good answers to these
questions.

- What do we need to know but don't?

- What do we know for sure, but the answer is unsatisfactory or
  unacceptable?

- What are all things we need but don't have?

- What are all the questions, unknowns, concerns, shortfalls,
  obstacles, or problems that could slow or stop your progress?

- Who has done this type of work before, and what were their
  problems, consequences, and effects?

- What are we forgetting to do?

Step 2. State each issue in one sentence.

Each *Unresolved Issue* should be stated in one sentence and answer these questions.

- What do we need specifically?
- How much (or how many) do we need, exactly?
- Why do we need it - the purpose?
- When's the latest we need it?
- Where do we need it?

For example, let's assume that you're responsible for a *Team-Building Session* for your company, but you still need a guest speaker. So, your *Unresolved Issue* might read:

> *"Need to identify and contract one guest speaker for the final dinner, on June 23, at our annual Team-Building Session at the Hilton Hotel no later than June 1."*

Step 3. Add it to the Unresolved Issues List.

Here's a simple table for your *Unresolved Issues*.

Unresolved Issues List				
Date	Action Item	Who	Deadline	Status/ Date
May 4	Need to identify and contract one guest speaker for the final dinner, on June 23, at our annual Team-Building Session at the Hilton Hotel no later than June 1.	Tom	June 23	Ongoing /May 10

Notice that this table captures the date the issue was identified (May 4), the action item stated in one sentence, Tom is responsible for resolving the issue, the deadline (DL) is June 23, and the current status with the date you last checked is "Ongoing/May 10." The reason for this much detail is to enable your boss and his boss to help you resolve your issues without asking you any questions.

Step 4. Provide a copy to your boss.

Always ensure your boss has a current copy of all your *Unresolved Issues*. If he doesn't have these details, he can't help you.

Step 5. Continue to eliminate each issue.

All *Unresolved Issues* should go on your list until two things happen:

- Until the answer is *known for certain*, the answer is a fact rather than an opinion or speculation.

- Until the answer is *acceptable to you*, meaning that it's no longer an issue.

Keep the issue on your list until the issue is both *"Known for Certain"* and *"Acceptable to You."*

Don't be surprised when one issue is resolved that several new issues appear. Just add them to your list and get as much help as you can to resolve each issue.

Step 6. Seek Assistance.

Also, discuss your *Unresolved Issues* during any future meetings or updates. Others at the meeting may be able to help you - but they need to know your issues.

Look, this technique is designed to help you get things done. No one can help you if they don't know your Unresolved Issues. So, don't let your pride or fear get in your way.

Always remember,

Asking for help is a sign of strength, not a sign of weakness.

Not knowing you need help is a sign of ignorance.

And needing help and not asking for it is a sign of stupidity.

So, don't get stuck on stupid!

When an issue is resolved, don't delete it from your list because you'll need it later for your *After-Action Review* (Chapter 37). Just record it as completed. When the issue is resolved, notify your boss.

Remember, the worst thing you could ever do is to conceal your Unresolved Issues from your boss.

This page is intentionally left blank.

26
BY ANTICIPATING
CONSEQUENCES AND EFFECTS

"The world is moved not only by the mighty shoves of heroes, but also by the aggregate of the tiny pushes of each honest worker."
- Helen Keller

Do you know how to anticipate and mitigate anything that could produce unexpected outcomes, causing delays or stoppage to your project?

By anticipating Unintended Consequences

Unintended Consequences are outcomes that aren't the outcomes expected from your project.

Unintended Consequences fall into three categories:

- **A positive**, unexpected benefit, which is usually referred to as serendipity or a windfall.

- **A negative**, unexpected problem like irrigation provides water for agriculture, and it could also lead to cholera.

- The consequence of **what others might say or do** is referred to as backlash, fallout, or blowback.

Here's an example of negative *Unintended Consequences*.

Can you tell what's wrong with this picture? Hint: Does Starbucks really suck?

Answer: The painters applied the Starbucks advertising on a delivery van with the doors closed. Unfortunately, they failed to consider the unintended consequences of what the van would look like when the side door was open. This is *Murphy's Law* at its best!

By anticipating Second and Third-Order Effects

Be sensitive to how your work affects others.

> ***Second and Third-Order Effects focus on how your work will affect others at different levels in your company.***

Different levels mean how your work will affect others in your unit, department, company, and suppliers.

Second and Third-Order Effects may also identify new resource requirements and cause changes to structures and procedures. For example, if you decide to change a supplier, the effects could be extensive.

- *Second-Order Effects* could require new ordering procedures to be created, which could cause delays.

- *Third-Order Effects* could require others to be retrained on new ordering procedures and software.

To anticipate *Second and Third-Order Effects* keep asking.

> ***Now, what? What's next? What're we forgetting? And what could happen or what might we need to do in 30, 60, or 90 days?***

How can you Anticipate Anything?

You're responsible for anticipating the consequences and effects of your work before starting.

But how can you do this when your crystal ball is no less clear than mine?

Method 1: Find others who have dealt with similar problems and ask:

- What problems, consequences, or effects did you have?

- Did everything go as planned? Any do-overs or surprises?

- What outside help did you need, and where did you get it?

- Anything or anyone you didn't have before starting?

- What was the most important and the most difficult task?

- How long did each task take, and what was the cost?
- Anything you'd start, stop, or change next time?
- Was everyone satisfied with the results?

Method 2: Vendors and Suppliers.

Contact vendors and suppliers who have worked with those who have dealt with the same or similar problems and ask the questions from Method 1. Also, which city, county, or state agency must inspect the problem to see if it meets the code?

Method 3: YouTube and Social Media.

Visit *YouTube* to search for related videos of others who have dealt with the same or similar problems. Then, get on social media and find people who have experienced projects or problems similar to yours. If you find someone, ask the questions from Method 1.

By making changes with CAUTION

Whenever a change is made, there are always consequences and effects. Just because everyone gets the change doesn't mean they understand it. The problem comes later when the consequences and effects start to appear, and everyone is shocked.

Here's a good example:

Bob was the Person-in-Charge of the company's Annual Team Building Session. Two days before the session, Bob's boss (the CFO) called and told him that the venue had been changed to a remote cabin where there was no electricity. Bob called John, the Key Player in-charge of food and beverages, to inform John of the change in venue and the lack of electricity.

The day before the session, Bob followed up with John and was shocked to find that John had not thought through the refrigeration requirements for the food and beverages. Since this was a three-day session, the change of venue not only required ice to be transported to the venue daily but coolers to store it.

John didn't recognize the need for ice, and Bob assumed John had it covered. As a result, the night before the session, both John and Bob spent several hours in the dark, scrambling around looking for coolers and bags of ice to fill them.

All this could have been avoided had John and Bob thought through the consequences and effects created by this last-minute change in venue by testing their assumptions and creating a Plan or Action to deal with it. Not to mention the need for a site recon and a new Risk Assessment (Chapter 32).

Murphy's Law on Consequences:

"There's never enough time to do it right, but there's always time to do it over."

27
BY BUILDING
CONSENSUS WITH A TEAM

"Unity is strength... when there is teamwork and collaboration,
wonderful things can be achieved."
- Mattie Stepanek

Do you know how to achieve agreement from all team members that they can support a proposal? Few people in the workforce today understand the meaning and value of collaborating to build consensus.

The process of building consensus starts with collaboration.

Collaboration is the process of working with others
to resolve a problem or achieve a goal.

Building consensus results from collaboration. Most people think that consensus means that everyone must like the proposal, the majority rules, or some other lame criteria - all of which are false.

Here's the truth!

Consensus is the desired end-product of
collaboration intended to achieve agreement from all
team members that they can support a proposal.

Support means that each member agrees that
the proposal will work and commits to doing
all they can to ensure its success.

If not, this is their chance to speak up! The process of building consensus gives every member the freedom to voice their agreements or disagreements before consensus is achieved. It's also intended to be inclusive, participatory, and cooperative, seeking opinions and input from all members.

Consensus uses common agreement to resolve mutually exclusive positions. It's not the majority rules, nor a popularity contest. It doesn't care whose proposal is being considered or if any member likes or dislikes the proposal. It only asks each member if they can support the proposal. If not, a valid reason must be provided.

VALID means that their reason must be either a better proposal or a fact and not an opinion.

Why is building consensus important?

To answer this question, I always ask,

What's the Greatest Hunger of the Human Heart?

What does every human being need to be fulfilled at work?

The Greatest Hunger of the Human Heart is to be NEEDED.

To be needed means:

- To be seen means to be included and validated.
- To be heard means to be listened to, understood, and appreciated.
- To be valued means to be recognized for their contributions.
- To be treated with respect and kindness because they matter.

The greatest hunger of the human heart is to be seen, heard, valued, and treated with respect and kindness because they matter.

If team members aren't allowed to *"speak their piece,"* you're telling them that they're not important and they don't matter. Not good! Do you feel needed where you work? Do those who work with you feel needed? Do you treat everyone with respect and kindness-no matter what?

Everyone needs to be engaged, involved, and have a say concerning the things that affect their wellbeing.

This is why consensus building is so powerful.

When's consensus needed?

Consensus is needed whenever you're trying to resolve a problem, create a plan, or make any change that affects the team.

What are the benefits of building consensus?

- Consensus building improves the proposal by using the wisdom and knowledge of the team.

- It uncovers any Unintended Consequences and Second and Third-Order Effects that could slow or stop the proposal.

- It builds trust and commitment from the team by engaging them and using their input.

Building consensus is far more important than achieving it because, in the end, everyone may not agree to support the proposal, but at least they've been included in the process.

Failure to build consensus will erode teamwork, commitment and cause the failure to consistently produce excellent results. Building consensus sounds easy, but it's not. However, it's worth it because, without their involvement, they'll never be committed! And without their commitment, you'll never be able to consistently produce excellent results!

By building Consensus

Here are two methods of building consensus:

- **Staffing a Proposal.** This means circulating a proposal document through all team members to obtain their concurrence or non-concurrence with comments.

- **Conducting a Team Meeting.** This method works best when the proposal is an important decision that's time-sensitive, involves major funding, and affects the entire team.

If this is the case, here are the most important steps to build consensus.

Step 1. Discuss the proposal.

Gather the team, either at one location or on a phone or video conference, and discuss the proposal.

- **If the proposal is a problem,** how was it discovered, how bad is it, and what're the risks if it continues unresolved? What's causing this problem? Is this the real problem or just a symptom? And how do we know for sure?

- **If the proposal is a goal,** why is it important? What's the intended benefit?

Step 2. Discuss the Solution.

If the solution is obvious, then work with the team to create the *Plan of Action* to implement the solution. If there could be several solutions, conduct a *Brainstorming Session* and select the best solution (Chapter 21).

Step 3. Anticipate the Consequences and Effects.

Once the solution has been identified, discuss the possible *Unintended Consequences* and *Second and Third-Order Effects* (Chapter 11).

Step 4. Eliminate all Unresolved Issues.

Discuss and identify all *Unresolved Issues* (any question, unknown, concern, shortfall, obstacle, or problem) that could slow or stop your progress (Chapter 10).

Step 5. Ask for Consensus.

Now, ask all team members if they can support the proposal. If not, why? Remember,

> **Support means that each member agrees that the proposal will work and commits to doing all they can to ensure its success.**

If all members agree, ask them to create the *Plan of Action* to implement the proposed solution. If any member has a valid reason for non-support, continue to Step 6.

By resolving Reasons for Non-Support

At this point, only valid reasons should be considered. However, real-life doesn't work that way. Members will always have concerns and opinions, and they need to be heard. Here are the most important steps.

Step 6. Deal with their concerns.

If a member has a concern or opinion that's not a fact, this is when things get interesting.

- If their concern is that it's **too costly**, what does he mean? Too costly compared to what? How can the cost be reduced or offset? What's the contingency plan if it does cost more?

- If their concern is that it **will take much longer**, what's he basing this on? What's the downside if it does take longer? What's our Contingency Plan if it does?

- If their concern is that it's **too risky**, what does he mean? Can it be mitigated? Can a contingency plan be created just in case?

Step 7. Convert Reasons to Risks.

Before continuing, exchange the term *"Reason"* for *"Risk."* This will make this process much easier to understand. And for each risk, there are two critical things you must consider, probability and impact.

Step 8. What's the Probability?

How likely is this risk to happen (Chapter 12)? If the probability is *Low*, place the risk, *On-Hold*. This means that it's been noted and set aside temporarily. If the probability is *Medium* to *High*, or you're unsure, continue to the next step.

Step 9. What's the Impact?

What's the Impact or Effect on the proposal when this risk happens (Chapter 12)? If the Impact is *Minor,* place the risk *On-Hold*. If the Impact is *Moderate* to *Significant*, or you're unsure, continue to Step10.

Step 10. Can the Risk be Mitigated?

- If the risk can be mitigated, create a *Contingency Plan* (Chapter 15).

- If the risk can't be mitigated, you still have three options (Chapter 14).

Remember, you don't need a consensus before sending the proposal to your boss for approval. However, you'll need to include all reasons for non-support and let your boss decide. All members don't have to like the solution! They just need to be able to support it.

By Staffing a Proposal

Here's another method of building consensus without a meeting.

Staffing is the process of circulating a proposal document to all team members to obtain their concurrence or non-concurrence with comments in writing.

This method works best in situations where the proposal is routine and not time-sensitive. The proposal document could be a procedure, plan, question, or idea. Here are the four most important steps.

Step 1. Provide the proposal document to all members.

Ensure each team member receives a copy of the proposal document. Ask each member for their concurrence or non-concurrence with comments. And don't forget to provide a deadline.

Step 2. Resolve non-concur comments.

When member comments are returned to you, you may need to visit some members privately to better understand their comments and determine if adjusting your proposal could lead to their concurrence. Remember, concurrence means that each member agrees that:

The proposal will work and commits to doing all they can to ensure its success.

If not, a valid reason must be provided, which means their non-concur comments must be a better proposal or a fact and not an opinion.

Step 3. Make changes.

If you need to make changes, you'll need to send the revised proposal to all members again for another review. And for the second review, ensure you highlight any changes made from the first review.

Step 4. Obtain approval.

Note: You don't need the concurrence of all team members before sending your proposal to your boss for approval, but you'll need their reasons for non-concurrence. Remember, building consensus should never be done in a vacuum. You need the feedback to help you see beyond your blind spots.

28
BY PROVIDING
ADVANCED WARNING

"History is a vast early warning system."
- Norman Cousins

Do you know how to ensure your team members and Key Players know what you're *planning and have sufficient time to respond rather than react?

How would you feel if your boss told you that you're flying to Europe tomorrow when he's known about it for a month?

A Key Player is anyone you're counting on to perform a task for your project to be a success.

Advanced Warning is informing all team members and Key Players of what you're planning, so they can plan.

The most important thing you can do for your team members and Key Players is to give them as much time as possible to plan and prepare by telling them what you're planning to do. You do this by providing as much Advanced Warning as you can.

In the **US Military**, it's called a *"Warning Order."* It includes an Objective statement from the Draft *Plan of Action* (POA), telling as many specifics as possible. For example, it should include the who, what, when, where, and why you're planning. It should also include when they can expect the final POA. Unless the task is time-sensitive, an email to each team member and Key Player should suffice. However, provide as much information as you can. If anything is unknown, list it as TBA (To Be Announced).

What's the "One-Third, Two-Thirds Rule?"

When planning a project, the rule states that if there are three weeks until a project starts, the first week is yours to create the Plan of Action and Backbrief your boss, and the two remaining weeks belong to your Key Players for their *planning and preparation.

*To learn more about **Planning**, available at **Amazon.com**, see page 5.

This page is intentionally left blank.

29

BY CONDUCTING AN
IN-PROGRESS REVIEW

"If I had to live my life again, I'd make the same mistakes, only sooner."
- Tallulah Bankhead.

How do you know if your project is progressing as planned and if it's ready to move to the next phase?

An In-Progress Review is a synchronization meeting conducted by the Project Manager with all Key Players present to collaborate and coordinate a project.

Normally, each major project will have at least two *IPRs* scheduled between phases of the project.

- **IPR 1** is normally scheduled at the halfway point of the time remaining (between the Planning and Preparation Phases).

- **IPR 2,** the second or last IPR, is normally scheduled 5-7 days before the project starts (between the Preparation and the Execution Phases).

IPRs essentially become *Milestones* (A tool used to mark specific points along a project timeline and focus on major progress phases that must be reached before moving forward).

What should be discussed during each IPR?

If this is your project, this is your opportunity to check if everyone involved, especially the *Key Players,* is on schedule, knows about all changes, and has no *Unresolved Issues* (Chapter 25).

- **Deliverables:** During the IPR, the project's current progress is addressed, and *deliverables* designated in the *POA* are presented. A *deliverable* is something tangible that proves that a Key Player has taken action designated in the *POA* (like a sales receipt, a purchase order, or diagram). If all *deliverables* are present, the project moves to the next phase. If all *deliverables* are not presented, the project is stopped (or delayed) until the boss becomes directly involved for explanations and gives the go-ahead.

- **Unintended Consequences and Second and third-Order Effects (Chapter 26).**

- **Unresolved Issues (Chapter 25).**

30
BY FOLLOWING UP
AND FOLLOWING-THROUGH

"Learning the secrets and skill of great No.2s
remains the surest path to becoming No. 1."
- David Heenan and Warren Bennis.

Do you know how to *Follow up* and *Follow-through* to increase your probability of success and enhance your effectiveness and credibility at work? Many mistakes and failures in business can be traced back to someone who failed to *Follow up or Follow-through.*

By Following up

Follow up is a subsequent action taken to check on the validity of an initial action.

And there are three situations where *Follow up* is needed.

Situation 1.
When someone fails to respond to your solicitation.

Using a sales example, if a prospect fails to respond to your solicitation or declines to do business with you, you still should *Follow up. Follow-up* means continuing to contact them until you receive a positive response. The secret is to continue to add value to the person you're trying to contact.

Situation 2.
When you're trying to contact someone to resolve a problem.

Here are the most important steps if you're trying to resolve a problem (like poor customer service, a faulty product, or a delayed order).

Step 1. Call to resolve the problem.

Record the date you called, whom you spoke with, and the response you received.

Step 2. Leave a detailed voicemail message.

If you get their voicemail, always leave a message giving the date, your name, company, phone number, a detailed description of the problem with its reference number, and a request for a return call.

Step 3. Document your actions.

Always document your *follow-up* action. This way, when your boss asks, you can show him your *"Action Log."*

Step 4. Show up in person.

After you've called three times with no response, show up in person and get your problem resolved.

Step 5. Add it to your Unresolved Issues List.

Until resolved, keep this issue on your *Unresolved Issues List* and ensure your boss has a current copy (Chapter 25).

Situation 3.
After delegating an assignment or making a reservation or appointment.

Follow up also means contacting someone a few days before the due date of your assignment, reservation or appointment to confirm it's still valid.

Delegating an assignment isn't abdication because the asker is still responsible and accountable for the end-result.

5% of delegating is asking someone to perform a task.

The other 95% is about following up to ensure it gets done.

A good 30% of the time, my reservations or appointments got lost. I assumed that all was good-to-go, and I was sadly mistaken.

Here's a great story of how it should be done

On June 1ˢᵗ, Joe was asked by his boss to set up a luncheon for 30 senior executives at the best steak house in town for June 15th.

This was two weeks before the luncheon when Joe made the initial reservation. He recorded the date, time, and the name of the person he spoke with on his Assignment Tracking Form (Appendix E).

On June 12th, a few days before the luncheon, as Joe was reviewing his Assignment Tracking Form, he decided to follow up, and here's how it went. Hi, this is Joe Sanchez from Trident Resources. I'm calling to follow up on the reservation for our company's luncheon for Thursday, June 15th, at 11:30 AM? Is everything still on track?

The scheduler said, "Joe, I don't have a reservation for your company. When did you make it, and whom did you speak with? After looking at his Assignment Tracking Form, Joe said, "I called two weeks ago, on June 1st, and I spoke to Carol Brown."

After a long pause, the scheduler continued, "Carol was let go two weeks ago. That may explain the problem. After another long pause, she said, "Joe, you're lucky. You called just in time. If you had waited another day, you'd be out of luck." After Joe's heart rate returned to normal, he was glad he documented all his phone calls and followed up when he did. If not, he would have had 30 senior executives standing around looking for a place to eat. Not good.

By Following-through

This is what your boss means when he says, *"Get back to me, let me know, or keep me in the loop."*

Follow-through is the process of returning to the asker, either face-to-face or on the phone, and reporting the status of their request.

There are two situations where *Follow-through* is needed.

Situation 1.
When your boss or customer asks you to do something.

When this happens, make sure you have a clear understanding of what the boss or customer wants to be done (the task) and when he needs it completed (the deadline). If you have any questions, ask! If you can't deliver, speak up! After completing the task, *Return and Report*, either face-to-face or on the phone.

Return and Report mean contacting the asker, either face-to-face or on the phone, to update the status of their request. If you can't complete the task as requested, return, either face-to-face or on the phone, and report the problem. Also, recommend what should be done to resolve the problem.

Returning and Reporting is the most important part of Following-through.

Situation 2.
When you ask a Direct Report to do something.

When you ask a Direct Report to do something, ensure you tell him WHAT you want to be done (the task) and WHEN you need it completed (the deadline).

Also, ask him to *Follow-through*. You may have to explain what you mean. Explain that you want him to *Return and Report*, either face-to-face or on the phone when the task is completed. If he can't complete the task, ask him to return, either face-to-face or on the phone, and report the problem and recommend what needs to be done to resolve it.

The most effective people I know, those at the *top of their game*, do something special.

They over-communicate!

They Follow-through even if they have nothing new.

This way, I know I wasn't forgotten!

When you *Follow-through*, you'll stand out above the rest.

Note: When you tell someone that *"I'm-on-it,"* you've just told them that you'll *Follow-through*.

31
BY MANAGING
RISK

There is only one big risk you should avoid at all costs,
and that is the risk of doing nothing."
- Denis Waitley

How do you manage the risk associated with your work?

Simply Stated, RISK is Uncertainty!

Managing anything requires the ability to anticipate and mitigate risk. You can't control everything that happens to you, but you can control your degree of preparation and how you respond.

Here are the most important things to consider when assessing risk.

1. Reduce the Risk of Failure.

By planning for risk to occur, you're decreasing your probability of failure, which increases your probability of success. Much of this is done every day in your company. It's called risk reduction, like having fire, theft, and liability insurance.

2. Understand that control is an illusion.

This simple prayer, which I learned during my recovery from alcoholism, helped me finally answer this life-altering question:

What are the only things in life I can
control and therefore change?

THE SERENITY PRAYER

"God, grant me the Serenity to

Accept the things I cannot change,

Courage to change the things I can,

and the Wisdom to know the difference

- Reinhold Niebuhr

And these answers changed my life forever.

**In this life,
You cannot control or change other people,
places, things, situations, or circumstances.**

**The only things you can control and therefore
change are your thoughts, words, and deeds.**

And all those years, I thought I could control and change other people. What a waste of time and energy. This may come as a shocking epiphany for many of you because you've probably made the same mistake.

*Yes, you can influence them, but you can't control
or change them. You can only control
and therefore change yourself.*

This concept is crucial because until you learn to truly control what you can control (your thoughts, words, and deeds), you'll never influence anyone to help you consistently produce excellent results.

3. Identify your Risk Goals.

When it comes to managing risk, you should always have two goals:

- Make the Risk LESS likely to happen, like putting training wheels on your child's bicycle.

- Make the Impact LESS severe when, and NOT if it happens, like requiring your child to wear a safety helmet.

4. Plan for both Anticipated and Unanticipated Risk.

In life, there are always two categories of risk:

- *Anticipated Risks* are those risks that include all the things that could *reasonably-go-wrong* (Chapter 31), including anything that could slow or stop your project or cause injury, illness, accident, death, security violations, property damage, or financial loss.

- *Unanticipated Risks* are those Risks that you could not possibly have predicted (Chapter 35).

5. Conduct a Risk Assessment.

With the help of your team, conduct a *Risk Assessment.*

Anticipated Risk comes in two forms:

- **Bad Internal Situations** are things that don't require a call to 911, like equipment breakdowns, people being late, cell phone batteries going dead, and other mistakes, defects, or errors.

- **Bad External Situations** are things that will require a call to 911, like fire, injuries, accidents, property damage, violence, or theft.

6. Assess the Impact and Probability.

For each Bad Situation, assess these two critical things:

- **Impact** means how this Bad Situation will affect your project and is rated as *Significant, Moderate, or Minor.* Based on your assessment, when, and not if, this Bad Situation happens, how serious will it affect your project?

- **Probability** means how likely is this Bad Situation to happen and is rated as *High, Medium, or Low.* Based on your assessment, how likely is this Bad Situation to occur?

7. Assess your Risk Options.

Option 1. AVOID the Risk.

In some cases, you may want to avoid the risk altogether. This could mean not getting involved or just deleting a high-risk activity. This is a good option when taking the risk involves no advantage or when the cost of mitigating isn't worth the risk.

However, when you avoid a potential risk entirely, you may miss an opportunity. So, do your *What if Analysis* to explore your options before deciding. To learn more, search *YouTube* for *"What if analysis on Excel."*

Option 2. SHARE the Risk!

You could decide to share the risk and the potential gain with others. For example, you share risks when you ensure your project site or partner with another company.

Option 3. ACCEPT the Risk.

This option is usually best under these conditions:

- When there's nothing you can do to prevent the risk.

- When the potential loss is less than the cost of insuring against the risk.

- When the potential gain is worth accepting the risk.

For example, you might accept the risk of a project launching late if the potential sales will still cover your costs.

8. Beware of Scope Creep.

Scope means the size of the project and its requirements, complexity, and goals. Scope creep occurs when others want to make changes to your project. So, negotiate these changes to gain either more time or more money, or both.

9. Create Contingency Plans.

The purpose of any *Contingency Plan* (Chapter 35) is to diminish the severity of a bad situation when it occurs. *Contingency Plans* need to be *Staffed* (Chapter 27) through all Key Players and approved by the boss.

10. Use Preventive Actions.

Mistakes are not a problem if they're caught before they get in front of your boss or the customer.

What *Assessment Systems* (Chapter 6) or procedures do you have to catch mistakes? Effective people anticipate and mitigate their risk by adding *Preventive Actions* to their *Project's Timetable* (Chapter 5).

32
BY CONDUCTING A
RISK ASSESSMENT

"Take risks: if you win, you will be happy;
if you lose, you will be wise."
- Unknown

Effective people know that conducting a good *Risk Assessment* is critical to their probability of success. You can't control everything that happens to you, but you can control your degree of preparation and how you respond. With the help of your team, conduct a good *Risk Assessment* by *Brainstorming* (Chapter 34) anything related to your work that could *reasonably-go-wrong.*

Here are the most important steps to conduct a good *Risk Assessment.*

Step 1. Anticipate the Physical Risks.

Have you inspected the site for anything that could cause an injury, accident, illness, or death? How about safety, sanitation, and access for those with disabilities - any risk there?

Step 2. Anticipate the Security Risks.

- For *cybersecurity*, what could cause a data breach, loss of personal info or intellectual property, or a disruption of services?

- For *physical security*, what could permit unauthorized access leading to theft or property damage?

Step 3. Anticipate the Financial Risk.

- What could cause financial loss through fraud, waste, or abuse?

- What insurance is needed, and is it current?

Step 4. Anticipate the Operational Risks.

- What's the *Impact* when these risks occur (Chapter 31)?

- What's the *Probability* that these risks will happen (Chapter 31)?

- How can these risks be mitigated (Chapter 33)?

- What's your *Contingency Plan* for when they do (Chapter 35)?

- Do your team members know how to take *Immediate Action* (Appendix B)?

- What assumptions are needed to move the work forward (Appendix D)?

- What *Preventive Actions* (Chapter 4) did you add to your *Plan of Action (POA) Timetable* (Chapter 5).

- Have you *Staffed* your POA (Chapter 27) with the team, and what was the result?

- What are you forgetting to do?

Step 5. Eliminate Unresolved Issues.

What are all the questions, unknowns, concerns, shortfalls, obstacles, or problems that could slow or stop our progress (Chapter 25)?

Step 6. Anticipate and Mitigate Unintended Consequences.

Unintended Consequences are the outcomes that aren't expected by your actions (Chapter 26).

Step 7. Anticipate Second and Third-Order Effects.

Second and Third-Order Effects focus on how your recommendations or decisions affect others at different levels in your organization (Chapter 26).

Step 8. Anticipate the Risk of Bad Situations.

- **Bad Internal Situations** are situations that *don't require a call to 911*, like equipment breakdowns, people being late, cell phone batteries going dead, mistakes, defects, or errors.

- **Bad External Situations** are situations that *require a call to 911*, like fire, injuries, accidents, property damage, violence, or theft (Chapter 33).

If you fail to conduct a good *Risk Assessment* before your next project, do so at your peril.

You've been WARNED!

33
BY MITIGATING THE RISK
TO BAD SITUATIONS

"If you are not living on the edge, you are taking up too much room."
- Jayne Howard

How do you mitigate the risks to anticipated bad situations? In business, there are two different types of risk: Internal and External.

By mitigating the Risk to Bad Internal Situations

This includes equipment breakdowns, people being late, cell phone batteries going dead, and other mistakes, defects, or errors.

Bad Internal Situations are situations
that don't require a call to 911.

Once you've determined everything that could *reasonably-go-wrong*, you're ready to mitigate the risks. Here are the most important steps.

Step 1. Brainstorm.

Conduct a *Brainstorming Session* to determine what actions are needed to respond to each bad situation (Appendix K).

Step 2. Create Contingency Plans.

Now that you've determined what actions are needed for each Bad Internal Situation, it's time to create a *CONPLAN* for each (Chapter 35).

Step 3. Rehearse each CONPLAN.

Rehearse each *CONPLAN* a few days before your project to identify any errors, omissions, or misunderstandings. Don't just ask people if they're ready. Ask them to show you that they're ready (Chapter 36).

Step 4. Eliminate All Unresolved Issues.

Continue to eliminate all *Unresolved Issues* by facilitating collaborative *problem-solving to build consensus (Chapter 25).

*To learn more about **Problem-Solving**, available at **Amazon.com,** see page 5.

By mitigating the Risk to Bad External Situations

The truth is that even though local first responders have more resources and training than you, you can still make the risk less likely to happen and make the impact less severe when it occurs.

Bad External Situations are those that require a call to 911.

Here are the most important steps to mitigate the risk of Bad External Situations.

Step 1. Assess the Risk of Fire.

Since most fires start as small fires, do you have more fire extinguishers on-site than you need? Do people know where they're located and how to use them? Have they been tested and inspected? Are there sufficient smoke detectors present and serviceable? Are there any local restrictions on burning, building fires, or fire warnings?

Step 2. Assess the Risk of Medical Issues.

Do you have first aid kits on-site, with staff trained on how to administer first aid? When were these kits last inspected and replenished? Can ambulances be located closer to your venue? Do you have staff trained to administer CPR? Do defibrillators be centrally located with staff trained in how to use them?

What about those who have food allergies and those allergic to bee stings? And how about mosquitos, the elderly, and the disabled? Are there any unsafe conditions that could lead to an injury or accident? Are there any unsanitary conditions that could lead to illness?

Step 3. Assess the Risk of Crime.

Whenever assessing the risk of crime, always consider:

- **Access control** means entry denial, metal detectors, gates, locks, keys, fences, barriers, checkpoints, firewalls, passwords, and badges.

- **Deterrence** means cameras, guards, dogs, signs, security lighting, punishment for violators, and barbed wire.

- **Early warning** means alarms, security systems, loudspeakers, intercom, flashing lights, police alerts, lockdowns, and sirens.

34
BY CONDUCTING A
BRAINSTORMING SESSION

"To win without risk is to triumph without glory."
- Pierre Corneille

How many times have you just assumed that you knew the BEST solution to a problem, only to find out later that you were wrong? Effective people know the value of *Brainstorming* when resolving problems and achieving goals.

Brainstorming is a group process of producing the most potential options to resolve a problem or achieve a goal.

Here are the most important steps.

Step 1. Pick your team.

Keep your group small (seven or less). If more than seven members, break them into smaller groups and compare the results.

Step 2. Use Mindstorming (Optional!).

The day before, give each team member a sealed envelope with instructions not to open it until they get home that night. Inside the envelope are instructions to conduct a *Mindstorming Exercise* by writing down many potential options for a problem. Also, ask them not to share their options before the meeting the next day.

Step 3. Prepare needed materials.

You'll need a blackboard, whiteboard, or some large sheets of paper on a vertical easel, wide-tipped markers to record all options for all to see.

Step 4. Decide how you'll participate.

Some members may not feel comfortable if you conduct the session. If you ever feel that your presence could diminish the team's effectiveness, find something else to do.

Step 5. Assign other duties.

If needed, select someone else to facilitate the *Brainstorming Session* and assign another member to act as the *Scribe* to record each option.

Step 6. Conduct the meeting.

A good *Brainstorming Session* should consist of these three phases.

Phase I. Capture All Options:

Limit this phase to 10-15 minutes or just enough time for each member to present their options. In this phase, you're looking for volume only. Judgment or criticism is reserved for the next phase.

Phase II. Discuss all Options:

After capturing everyone's options, this phase is where discussion is *encouraged, and options are consolidated.

Phase III. Validate each Option by using the *"Common-Sense Test:"*

This phase is designed to assess the validity of each option by using the *Common-Sense Test*. This test asks five questions about each option to qualify it as a valid option. If any option receives a *"No"* or *"we're not sure"* answer, it's eliminated.

> **1. Is it Suitable?** Does the option solve the problem, and is it legal and ethical?
>
> **2. Is it Feasible?** Does it fit within available or easily acquirable resources?
>
> **3. Is it Acceptable?** Is it worth the cost and the risk?
>
> **4. Is it Distinguishable?** Does it differ significantly from other options?
>
> **5. Is it Complete?** Does it solve the problem from start to finish?

Step 7. Select the Best.

In the end, you should have a list of valid options that require further research to help you select the best option. *Brainstorming* helps build commitment. Since you've included the team in the selection process, they'll be more committed to implementing the best option.

Involvement builds commitment, and commitment is critical to the consistent production of excellent results.

*To learn more about **Motivating**, available at **Amazon.com,** see page 5.

35
BY CREATING
CONTINGENCY PLANS

"If you don't risk anything you risk even more."
- Erica Jong

Do you know how to create a plan to respond to anticipated bad situations?

By creating a Contingency Plan

A Contingency Plan (or CONPLAN) is a Plan of Action that assumes that an anticipated bad situation has occurred.

Have you ever been involved with a project when things went wrong? What did you do? Was there a *Contingency Plan,* and was it rehearsed*?*

A *CONPLAN* is only executed when something bad happens. Being prepared is the key! What's your plan? Remember,

Many bad situations never become a problem

because someone knew what to do and

had the resources to respond.

Here are the most important steps.

Step 1. Collaborate.

Once you've identified all the bad things that could *reasonably-go-wrong,* collaborate with your team to determine what actions should be taken in response.

Step 2. Assess the Impact.

Impact means how this Bad Situation will affect your project and is rated as *Significant, Moderate, or Minor.* Based on your assessment, when, and not if, this Bad Situation happens, how serious will it affect your project?

Step 3. Assess the Probability.

Probability means how likely is this Bad Situation to happen and is rated as *High, Medium, or Low.* So, based on your assessment, how likely is this Bad Situation to occur?

If you have a bad situation with a Significant Impact and a High Probability of occurring, you'll need lots of help.

Step 4. Create a CONPLAN.

Once you've identified the actions that should be taken, create a CONPLAN to deal with each Bad Situation. Each CONPLAN uses the same format as a *Plan of Action* but begins with an assumption.

This assumption is the Bad Situation that you and your team have already anticipated. Your CONPLAN tells the reader exactly what to do when the assumption becomes true. It also lists what's needed, where it's stored, and how to use it.

Let's assume that you were assigned as the Project Manager for your company's *Team Building Session* in Buffalo, NY, in January. You and your team have already anticipated three Bad Internal Situations that could *reasonably-go-wrong* with your project.

- **For guests arriving late,** you assessed the Impact to be *Significant* because the Team Building Session won't be effective without all guests. However, you assessed your probability to be *Medium* because of the weather in Buffalo this time of year. So, for guests arriving late, you intend to use CONPLAN A.

- **For transporting guests to the resort,** you assessed the Impact to be *Moderate* because of the weather, the fact that the resort is 27 miles away, and that delays will disrupt the success of the team building session. And you assessed the probability to be *Medium* because you know that the weather in Buffalo this time of year is always a challenge. So, for Transporting guests to the resort, you intend to use CONPLAN B.

- **For lost baggage,** you assessed the Impact to be *Minor* because your activity can still go on regardless. However, you assessed the Probability to be *High* because the airlines in the winter have a history of losing luggage. So, for lost baggage, you intend to use CONPLAN C.

Step 5. Create your Risk Matrix.

Here's an example of a *Risk Matrix*.

Risk Matrix for Team Building Session			
BAD SITUATION	**IMPACT**	**PROBABILITY**	**CONPLAN**
Guests Arriving Late	Significant (8-10)	Medium (4-7)	A
Transport to Resort	Moderate (4-7)	Medium (4-7)	B
Lost Baggage	Minor (1-3)	High (8-10)	C

Notice that this simple table shows all Bad Internal Situations, their Impact, Probability, and which CONPLAN to use.

Note: The risk numbers 1 through 10 above are used to help create your *Risk Threshold*.

Step 6. Assess your Risk Threshold.

Here's an example of a *Risk Threshold Table*.

Risk Threshold = Impact X Probability.		
Risk Rating	**Risk Range**	**Remarks**
CRITICAL	50 or higher	The acceptable risk threshold for safety and health should always be lower than your financial or operational risks.
MEDIUM	16 to 49	
LOW	15 or Lower	

Notice that this table shows that a *risk threshold*, rated from critical to medium to low, is the sum of the impact times the probability. Knowing your risk threshold is important because your acceptable safety and health risk threshold should always be lower than your financial or operational risks.

Ideally, you should be doing all you can to reduce your risk. And if you can't, you'll need a good CONPLAN ready to respond.

Step 7. Staff your CONPLANs.

Staff your CONPLANs through all Key Players for their concurrence or non-concurrence with comments (Chapter 27).

Step 8. Obtain Approval.

Present your CONPLANs to your boss for approval with all the comments from your Key Players attached.

Step 9. Distribute your CONPLANs.

Once approved, ensure that all Key Players have a copy of all CONPLANs well before the project starts.

Step 10. Rehearse your CONPLANs.

A few days before your project starts, rehearse your CONPLANs with all Key Players (Chapter 36).

By creating an Unanticipated Situation Plan

Do you know how to create a plan to respond to unanticipated bad situations?

An Unanticipated Situation Plan is a Contingency Plan that assumes that an unanticipated bad situation will occur.

When unanticipated bad situations occur, what do you do? Is that even possible?

Preparing for *Unanticipated Bad Situations* requires a different level of thinking and preparation. Regardless of how well you plan, you'll always encounter bad situations that you did not, nor could not have anticipated. So, what do you do?

As a Project Manager, what will you do when an *Unanticipated Bad Situation* occurs on your watch? Your boss is counting on you to do everything you can to save, salvage, or secure your project.

You can't control everything that happens to you.

But you can control your degree of preparation and how you respond to them.

You already know that many Bad Situations never become problems because someone responded to them swiftly and decisively. They had

Assessment Systems (Chapter 6) and people in place to respond to these situations when they occurred. They saved the day!

But how did they do it? They did it by creating an *Unanticipated Situation Plan,* a special *Contingency Plan* that focuses on *Unanticipated Risk.*

Here are three special techniques that will help you prepare for and respond to *Unanticipated Bad Situations.*

1. Create a Quick Response Team (or QRT).

A *QRT* is a team specifically trained and equipped (with vehicle, keys, access codes, cash, and credit cards) on *Stand-by* (they have no other duties and are ready to respond, 24/7). Provide a sketch map to all *QRT* members that shows all locations near or at the site as reference points.

2. Use a Priority Response System.

The system is a cellphone protocol that requires that all Key Players:

- Respond to their cell phone before the second ring.
- Have extra batteries and car chargers easily available.
- Carry their cell phone on their person 24/7.
- Never let incoming calls from you go to voicemail.
- Have all contact numbers of all Key Players on their phones.
- Limit their outgoing calls to ensure they're able to respond.

This system is only effective if everyone plays by these rules. This is why it should be rehearsed. When you call, you need the Key Player to answer before the second ring - no excuses.

3. Create a Pre-Stocking Site.

This site is stocked with any materials, equipment, and supplies that could cause a delay or stoppage of your project.

- Do you have backup bulbs, projectors, and extension cords?
- Do you have backup batteries and AC and DC chargers?
- Where will these items be located?
- Do your boss, and all Key Players know this location?

Have one trusted Key Player responsible for this site, ready to deliver what, when, and where it's needed. Also, this site could be mobile, like a van or truck pre-positioned at or near the site, as needed.

Always be prepared to take *Immediate Action* (Appendix B).

By creating a Mitigation Plan

No one likes being on a project when things are going badly. So, how can you get the project back *on track*?

A Mitigation Plan is a POA designed to get a project back on-track by eliminating, consolidating, or rescheduling certain tasks to finish close to the originally planned date.

Here are the most important questions to ask if you ever have a project in trouble:

- Are there any tasks that can be eliminated, combined, **or** compressed?

- Is there *Slack Time* that can be used?

- Can anything be done simultaneously (or done *off-line*)?

- Do you need more people? Can overtime help?

- Should you go to a second shift or run 24-hours?

- Can working weekends and holidays help?

- Can the scope (size, requirements, complexity, goals) be reduced?

- Can the end time be moved to allow a successful completion?

Slack time: The amount of time in a schedule that a task can be delayed without causing a delay to other tasks or the project's completion date.

Getting behind schedule isn't fun. So, how does any project get thirty days behind? Answer: one day at a time, repeated thirty times. So, what's the message here? Don't get behind in the first place!

For those of you who think you'll never have to create a *Mitigation Plan* in your lifetime, think again. If you have a plan for getting your college education, MBA, or a Ph.D., what happens if you must take a year off? It's called a *Mitigation Plan* to help you pick up the pieces and move forward.

36
BY CONDUCTING A
REHEARSAL

"Take calculated risks. That is quite different from being rash."
- George S. Patton

Do you know how to uncover and correct any pre-problems that could slow or stop your project?

By Rehearsing

A Rehearsal is the process of reviewing (looking at) the results of others before they get in front of your boss to ensure all Pre-Problems (mistakes, defects, shortfalls, omissions, or errors) have been resolved.

The type of rehearsal I'm referring to here is to examine everything concerning your project BEFORE your boss sees it. How hard is that?

Why do you think weddings have rehearsals?

Do you have the ring, know where to stand, know what to say, and know the sequence of what's going to happen next? And why does it matter? Who wants it to be perfect? Enough said. What do you need to see, test, or practice a few days before your project starts?

Get a Clue! Even criminals have rehearsals because they know the consequences if they don't.

Rehearsals include things like previews, layouts, practice, a sand-table, or white-board walk-throughs. They also include demonstrations, role-playing, document reviews, and testing. And when your rehearsal uncovers a flaw, have it fixed and have another rehearsal.

Caution! Never ask people, *"are you ready?"* Instead, say, *"Show me that you're ready. I want to see it!"* What's stopping you?

Look, I can't tell you how many times I've been burned by people who've said to me that they were ready when they weren't. So, do yourself a favor. If this is your project, your job is to check. That means looking at everything before it gets in front of your boss.

By Practicing

As a child, I was told that *"Practice makes perfect."* As an adult, I learned that this was false. So, instead, it should be,

"Perfect practice makes perfect."

If you're practicing the wrong way, your results will suffer. That's why you always need a coach, someone who can show you how it should be done correctly to achieve the best result.

My favorite practice quote comes from **Coach Paul *"Bear"* Bryant**.

> ***"It's not the will to win that matters – everyone has that.***
> ***It's the will to prepare (or practice) to win that matters."***

It's no wonder Coach Bryant amassed six national championships and thirteen conference championships as the head coach of the University of Alabama's football team.

Growing up, I also learned that to be the best, I needed to *"Practice until I got it right."* However, much later in life, I found that to master anything, I needed to

"Practice until I couldn't get it wrong."

The best example of this comes from **Mary Lou Retton,** who won the gold medal in the 1984 Olympics in LA. She scored a perfect 10 in the vault competition.

After that vault, she asked the judges if she could do it again to show it wasn't just a lucky vault. Her score was another perfect 10. More impressive was that she was a sophomore in high school, had recently had leg surgery, and won two silver medals and two bronze medals.

Her performance was historic because she was the first-ever American woman to win the all-around gold medal at the Olympics, making her the most popular athlete in the US.

37

BY CONDUCTING AN
AFTER-ACTION REVIEW

"We don't have a crisis of leadership in Washington.
We have a crisis of followership."
- Jonathan Rauch

How can you enhance your performance and the performance of your team? One way is to use *After-Action Reviews.*

An After-Action Review (AAR) is a professional discussion conducted after an activity, with all members present, seeking ways to consistently improve the way things are done.

AARs should be conducted both during (at the end of each day) and the day after an activity (project, objective, or goal) by measuring the difference between what was supposed to happen (the Plan) vs. what did happen (Behavior and Results). Thus, AARs observe, measure, record, and assess an activity or process from start to finish to examine both the results and the behavior of those involved.

The purpose of an AAR is to:

- Capture and share intuition by asking HOW and WHY questions.

- Attempt to discover WHY things happen and how to get better.

- Help members understand HOW and WHY decisions are made.

- Encourage members to become *self-correcting* and more *aware of how their behavior affects others (Appendix F).

- Capture *Lessons Learned* to integrate into future operations.

Here are the four most important steps to conducting an AAR:

Step 1. The Objective.

Before the activity (project, objective, or goal): What are we trying to achieve? What performance standards and results are desired? Who and what will be observed, and how will it be measured?

*To learn more about *Awareness*, available at **Amazon.com,** see page 5.

Step 2. The Results and Behavior.

During the activity: What happened? What was observed and measured? What are the facts?

Step 3. The Assessment.

After the activity: Did things go as expected? Were there any surprises? If the result wasn't what we expected, what should be started, stopped, or changed to achieve a better result? WHY and HOW did we do what we did?

Step 4. The Lessons Learned.

What did we learn that can help us do better next time?

By using Informal After-Action Reviews

Let's assume that you're the Project Manager for a four-day Trade Show and you have three team members.

The week before the show, you and your boss sat down to discuss the plan and its objective. Why are we attending this show? What's the ideal outcome you'd like to see? How will this outcome be measured? After finishing with your boss, you met with your team and briefed them on the plan. Fast forward to the end of the first day of the show. You assembled your team and asked, what did we learn today that can make us better tomorrow?

One team member said it would have been nice to have some bottled water in our booth. A second member said, we also need a lunch schedule, so everyone has a chance to eat. Also, we're running low on our advertising brochures. You then asked one team member to provide bottled water in the booth every day. Then you asked another member to set up a lunch schedule for each day. And finally, you called your boss and asked him to overnight a bunch of advertising brochures. You also conducted an informal review at the end of each day with the goal of continuous improvement.

The day after the trade show, you gathered your team together and asked if we accomplished our goal? Did everything go as planned? Were there any surprises? What did we learn that could make the next Trade Show better? You then added all comments to your After-Action Report so next year's Trade Show can be even better. How hard was that?

38
BY ASSESSING A
PROJECT'S SUCCESS

"There are no secrets to success. It is the result of preparation,
hard work, and learning from failure."
- Colin Powell

Have you ever completed a project and wondered if the project was perceived as a success by your boss? Did you remember to negotiate this before you began the project?

Before determining how success is measured, let's go back to the beginning when the project was first assigned to you. You should have asked this question of your boss during your *Backbriefing*. Negotiate these details in advance on how success will be measured (like the amount of money donated, number of participants, customer feedback, a survey or measured against previous projects) and who's doing the measuring?

How can you determine if your project met its objective?

- Was it completed within budget, on-time, and to the satisfaction of the boss and customers?

- Conduct an informal *After-Action Review* (AAR) (Chapter 37) and ask the *Key Players* (anyone who must take action for the project to be a success)

- Compare the <u>actual</u> end-state to the <u>desired</u> end-state and ensure your boss is there.

- Ask a disinterested third party to observe and comment

- Administer a survey at the end of the project or ask participants individually.

How do you administer a Survey?

Have you ever wondered how the participants felt about a specific project since you could only speak with a few? For those whom you spoke to, how do you know they were telling you the truth? Administering a survey is a better way to get the truth and find out what people really felt.

In addition, administering a survey is a great way to anonymously receive feedback on how to improve your project in the future. It's also a great way to confirm or deny whether your project accomplished its intended objective.

If you use a survey and build upon it, you'll have another tool to help you. Surveys measure attitudes and provide credibility as to whether a project still provides *value-added*. This will come in handy at budget time to either kill or continue a project's funding.

Surveys are also great vehicles for tracking trends (Appendix E). For example, if you conducted your survey last year, you can administer the same survey every year and look for trends. Additionally, surveys, because they're anonymous, help justify what members really want, their attitudes, and opinions. This can be used as justification that something needs to be added, deleted, or changed. The feedback you'll receive is priceless. Don't assume you have all the answers.

What are subjective vs. objective measurements?

Not everything in life is measured objectively (with numbers and metrics). Many projects don't lend themselves to metrics and are measured subjectively.

Subjective measurements include:

Green, Yellow, Red / Go, No-go / Satisfactory – Unsatisfactory / Meets Standard vs. Needs work / Poor - Average - Above Average - Excellent – Outstanding / Good - Better – Best.

Tip:

The best surveys let you answer a statement using a range of responses. This method helps you track trends: opinions or attitudes.

For example:

1. My manager is supportive.

( ) Strongly Agree, ( ) Agree, ( ) No Opinion, ( ) Disagree, ( ) Strongly Disagree.

Each response can be assigned a numerical value: Strongly Agree = 10, Strongly Disagree = 0. If you administer the same survey every year, you can track the total score for each statement to see if your member's or customer's opinions are getting better (higher score) or worse (lower score).

39
BY LEARNING FROM
MISTAKES AND FAILURE

"If you're not making mistakes, then you're not doing anything.
I'm positive that a doer makes mistakes."
- John Wooden

Will you make mistakes and have failures in your lifetime? You bet lots of them. But that's how we all learn. So, how can you learn from mistakes and failure? Effective people know that the only thing that matters is what you learned for the next time.

What's Failure?

The dictionary defines failure as:

"The state or condition of not meeting a desirable or intended
goal and may be viewed as the opposite of success."

Failure is a relative term. It's viewed differently depending on your situation and who's doing the viewing. For example, failure to a baseball player may be striking out, but failure to his coach might be losing the game.

In the Business World, your goals will come from your boss. Did you accomplish the goals you were assigned? Did you achieve the result you wanted? If not, why?

The only important question is, what did you learn that can make you better next time? I used to think that there was no such thing as failure (it didn't exist) as long as you never gave up. But this is only partially true and sends the wrong message.

You'll experience mistakes and failures in your life. The trick is not to let them define you.

Instead, let them Refine you and make you stronger!

The past doesn't equal the future. So learn what you need to learn and move on!

What's the difference between a failure and an unsuccessful attempt?

- **Failure** needs a substantial loss (like money, time, or reputation).

- **An Unsuccessful Attempt** means that your last attempt did not achieve the desired result.

However, if you can make another attempt, did you learn why the last attempt was unsuccessful? Do you know what changes need to be made for your next attempt to be successful?

The example most often used comes from the story of **Thomas Edison** and his 10,000 attempts to create the incandescent light bulb. Just remember, *Edison* could make as many attempts as he needed until he was successful because he wasn't paying for each attempt. His investors were paying the bills. Most people don't have that luxury.

Failure only exists if there's a loss.

The bigger the loss, the bigger the failure.

What's Failure in the Real World?

There are two types of failure which are commonly misunderstood:

- **Personal failure:** This is an unsuccessful attempt at accomplishing your personal goal and includes a:

  - ✓ **Failure to try.** This is never setting goals or never attempting to accomplish anything.

  - ✓ **Failure to keep trying.** This means that after an unsuccessful initial attempt, you failed to learn from your mistakes, make the changes needed, find a different way to get there, or make another attempt.

  - ✓ **Substantial Loss.** This is a loss of your wealth, relationships, health, *character, or reputation.

- **Company failure:** This is a failure to accomplish an assigned goal, resulting in losing anything your boss couldn't afford to lose.

*To learn more about **Character**, available at **Amazon.com,** see page 5.

Let's examine what should happen BEFORE you attempt to accomplish any goal.

Before the Attempt

Step 1. What's the Risk?

Conduct a *Risk Assessment* to look for all the things that could reasonably go wrong during your attempt. Then, collaborate to assess all your safety, security, financial, and operational risk and how they can be mitigated.

Step 2. How many attempts?

If you know you'll only get one attempt, make it count! But, on the other hand, if you know you'll get as many attempts as you need, then the only risk is the cost of each additional attempt. Remember *Edison?*

Step 3. What's the cost?

- **Cost:** What will it cost to make this attempt (how much time, money, or effort will it take)?

- **Opportunity Costs:** What are you losing by not using other alternatives?

Step 4. What if you're wrong?

Can everyone live with an unsuccessful attempt?

Step 5. What are the benefits?

What benefits will you receive if your attempt is successful?

Step 6. Is the benefit worth the cost?

- **If Yes:** Continue to create your *Plan of Action.*

- **If No or Unsure:** Work hard to mitigate your Risk. Then, conduct another Cost/Benefit Analysis.

Step 7. What's your Assessment System?

An *Assessment System* is a series of procedures designed to measure the most critical parameters of your attempt to determine what went wrong, right, and why (Chapter 6)? How will the attempt be measured? How do you know when it's time to *pull-the-plug?*

After the Attempt

Let's examine what should happen AFTER your attempt.

Step 8. Was the attempt a complete success?

- **If Yes:** Congrats! What's next?

- **If No:** If your attempt was unsuccessful, was there a loss?

  - ✓ If there was **NO loss**, what did you learn, and what changes need to be made? Never give up! Just find another way to get there.

  - ✓ **If there was a loss**, now you have a real failure. The greater the loss, the greater the failure.

Step 9. What did you learn from your Assessment System (Chapter 6)?

- What went wrong, right, and why?

- What needs to change to make your next attempt a success?

- How will you know when it's time to *pull-the-plug*?

The lesson may have been painful, but don't throw the learning away. Mistakes and failures can be your best teacher, but only if you remember the lesson. Now what? Well, that depends on you!

Is Failure Fatal?

"Failure is not fatal, but failure to change might be."
- John Wooden

Assuming your attempt resulted in a loss, it's not the end of your life or your career. And, sometimes, getting close is good enough. So, assess what happened, what you learned, and get *back-in-the-game!*

Never give up! Just find another way to get there.

Never Stop Learning!

40
BY DEMONSTRATING
GOOD JUDGMENT

"Experience is simply the name we give our mistakes."
- Oscar Wilde

In your attempt to save time, do you rush and make snap decisions without considering the consequences?

Good judgment is your ability to bring together reason and wisdom to analyze a situation, explore your options, select a course of action, and take action.

Good judgment isn't about being smart or about making good decisions.

The essence of good judgment is about learning from past mistakes.

It's about using your *Assessment Systems* (Chapter 6) to ensure you don't repeat the same mistakes and increase the probability of success of your next attempt.

Judgment is less about getting it right and more about what it takes to learn what went wrong.

Some of your decisions will result in *Unintended Consequences*. To add to this uncertainty, you'll soon discover that your decisions aren't always about what's good or bad. Often, they're about choosing between good, better, and best. All decisions have consequences, which you won't see in advance. But experience teaches that they'll come due someday.

Where do good decisions come from?

Good decisions don't happen by accident.

- Good decisions come from good judgment.

- Good judgment comes from failure.

- Failure comes from mistakes.

- Mistakes come from bad decisions.

- Bad decisions come from bad judgment.

- Bad judgment comes from a lack of experience.
- Lack of experience comes from:
  - ✓ Having little time invested in the job.
  - ✓ Not learning from your mistakes.
  - ✓ Not learning from the mistakes of others.
  - ✓ Making quick decisions when you have more time.
  - ✓ A failure to venture outside your comfort zone.

*Mistakes, as long as you learn from them,
are the building blocks of greatness.*

How can you learn from the mistakes of others?

Learning from the mistakes of others only happens if you're paying attention. The truth is that anyone can cut their learning curve and gain years of valuable experience by using this simple principle:

*There are only two ways to learn anything in life, either
by trial and error or by modeling the best practices.*

While it's important to learn from your mistakes, it's a lot easier to learn from the mistakes of others.

How can Modeling help you?

*Experience is the toughest teacher because it gives
the test first and the knowledge second.*

Modeling a better teacher because it gives you the knowledge, so you're better prepared for the test.

**Modeling is the process of learning from those
who've already achieved success.**

It also means learning by copying the behavior of those who've already experienced the mistakes and failures on their journey to success (Chapter 39). You can avoid the same mistakes and failures by learning, applying, and sharing what you'll learn here. Each new skill learned builds on the previous, and the compound effect is career-changing.

41
BY KNOWING WHEN TO
ACT, WAIT OR WALK AWAY

"You got to know when to hold 'em. Know when to fold 'em.
Know when to walk away and know when to run."
- Kenny Rogers, The Gambler.

When faced with a problem, how do you know what to do? For every problem you'll face, you'll normally have three choices of how to respond:

You can act, wait, or walk away.

When faced with a problem, can't you just do nothing? Sure. Think about it. You have this option every time you're faced with a problem. Do some problems sometimes correct themselves by doing nothing? Yes. Do some problems get worse by taking action rather than doing nothing? You bet!

Remember, doing nothing is deciding by default.

Are there some problems that are better left alone? Sure. Just ask any Firefighter. Most of the time, all they can do is contain the fire and just let it burn itself out; let *it burn-to-the-ground.* If you feel this is your best choice, among all the choices you have at the time, then do nothing – let it *burn-to-the-ground.*

However, doing nothing and waiting
are two different options.

When faced with any problem, use these steps to guide your response.

Step 1: Should I Act NOW?

Before deciding, answer these questions?

- Can this problem be resolved by calling 911? If Yes, call!

- Will acting now save lives or avoid further damage?

    ✓ If Yes, take *Immediate Action* (Appendix B).

    ✓ If No to both questions, continue to Step 2.

Step 2: Is this my problem?

Is this my problem or someone else's?

- Who has the most to gain or lose from its resolution?
- Who's affected by this problem?

If this problem isn't your problem, why are you trying to solve it? Just report it to your boss and walk away. If this is your problem, continue to the next step.

Step 3: Should I act now or wait?

How urgent is this problem?

- How important or urgent is this problem and why?
- What must happen before I'm forced to act?
- What are the consequences if this problem remains unresolved?
- What's the downside of waiting?

How much time do I have?

- How long do I have before this problem becomes a crisis?
- How long do I have before I'm forced to act?
- When's it too late to act?

Based on your answers to the above questions, use the *Decision Support Template* below to guide your decision.

Here's an example of a *Decision Support Template*: Time vs. Urgency.

Decision Support Matrix		Time to Decide?	
		Little Time	Enough Time
Urgency?	Urgent	1	2
	Not Urgent	3	4

Here's what the numbers mean:

1. If this problem is urgent and you have little time to decide, take *Immediate Action* (Appendix B) and develop a mental *Plan of Action* before acting (Appendix A). See CONPLAN 1.

2. If this problem is urgent and you have enough time, take Step 4. Prepare to act after completing your *Plan of Action*. Keep your boss informed. See CONPLAN 2.

3. If this problem isn't urgent and you have little time to decide, wait, continue to monitor the situation, create your *Plan of Action*, and keep your boss informed. See CONPLAN 3.

4. If this problem isn't urgent and you have enough time to act, continue to monitor the situation, create your *Plan of Action*, and update your boss. See CONPLAN 4.

Also, document what happened, when, and who took what action to resolve the problem for investigative or legal purposes later.

Step 4: Create your Plan of Action.

See Appendix A.

Note: You're responsible for anticipating your work's consequences and effects BEFORE deciding (Chapter 26).

Other Things to Consider

When's the best time to decide?

> *"The key is not to make quick decisions,*
> *but to make timely decisions."*
> *- Colin Powell*

Do you have to make the decision right now? This classic answer is usually, No! This is rarely necessary. Resist the impulse of making a snap decision when there's no need to do so. Normally, you'll have sufficient time to decide.

A good rule of thumb is to decide after acquiring **40-70%** of the information you need. Mistakes, as long as you learn from them, are the building blocks of greatness. If it turns out bad, adjust, and remember what you've learned for next time.

Who's the Best Person to decide?

First, the boss decides! Or, at least, the boss should take responsibility and ownership of his team's decisions, especially if it turns out bad. Ask members for their input before you decide. Also, if the decision affects everyone in your team, why can't all members be given a chance to concur or non-concur with reasons (Chapter 27)?

Does the Best Decision always produce the Best Outcome?

There's a big difference between your decision and the result or outcome of your decision. You could be the most experienced decision-maker on the planet, and you could make the best decision, but there's no guarantee that your problem will be resolved or the best outcome will be achieved. You can make a good decision, and the results could still be bad. The situation and facts available when you first decided could (and probably will) change over time. What was good today could turn out to be bad tomorrow.

Do you need your Boss's Approval?

Have you ever been in a situation where you were waiting for your boss's approval? Why are you asking for approval if the problem is internal, doesn't require additional resources you don't have, and isn't in conflict with any internal standards? Of course, that's what your boss is paying you to do. But do let him know.

Sometimes it's easier to ask forgiveness than permission.

Or, if you're in doubt, tell your boss when you'll be making your decision (like the end of the week), and if you don't hear from him before that time, you'll be moving forward. Don't forget to assess the consequences and effects of your actions.

What if a Direct Reports recommends a change?

One of the best bosses I ever worked with once said,

> **"If I can't give you a good reason not to make the change; I'll approve it."**

Yes, they still had to create a *Decision Paper* (Appendix C), build consensus with the team (Chapter 27), and present it to the team for a final discussion before approval. However, this gave the team the freedom they needed to make things better.

APPENDIX A:
CREATE
A PLAN OF ACTION

Here's a great checklist to use when creating your next *Plan of Action*.

OBJECTIVE (Who, What, Where, When, and Why?)

- What's my access to sources of info, and who's this project for?
- Where is this project being conducted?
- Why is this project being done?
- How important is this project, and to whom is it important?
- How will success be measured, and who will measure it?
- What's the requirement, scope, and complexity of work?
- What's the limit of my authority (decisions, delegate, spend $, hire, and fire)?
- Does someone with authority approve this?
- When does this project start and end?
- What's the most important task for this project to be a success?
- Who has done this task before, and what were their problems, consequences, and effects?
- What must be ordered or started now?

METHODS (How)

- How should we do it? What are all our options, which is best?
- What needs to happen during the four phases of this project?
- What're all the tasks involved, and who are responsible for performing each task (Key Player)?
- What must be done before, during, and after the project?
- What specific instructions do we have for those delegated a task?
- How many are expected to attend or are affected by this?
- What're our restrictions (can't do) and imperatives (must do)?

- Who has done this or a similar type of project before?

- How will this project be advertised or promoted?

- What are my responsibilities, expectations, duties, constraints, authority, and standards?

- Who're the most important people to talk to right now?

- What're the consequences if this turns out unsuccessful?

TIMETABLE (Chapter 5)

- Planning backward from today, when are the Planning, Preparing, Executing, and Assessment Phases?

- When's the *Backbriefing?*

- What's the *Project Update Briefing* schedule?

- Which *Preventive Actions* must be done during each phase?

- How long will each task take, and what's the best sequence of these tasks and *Preventive Actions?*

- Which tasks can't start or finish without another task starting or finishing? (Dependent tasks)

- Which task needs to be started right now?

- What's the detailed schedule, program, and calendar?

- When's the rehearsal, and what will be rehearsed?

- What else is going on in the company or *community at the same time? What happened last year at this time?

*Do you really want your project to go on at the same time as Spring Break, the Superbowl, or a Presidential Election Voting Day?

RESOURCES

- What resources are most important for the success of this project?

- How much of each resource is needed, when, and where?

- Who's responsible (Key Player) for providing these resources?

- When's the latest time we need these resources delivered?

- Who's paying for this, and what must be ordered now?

- What skills, attitudes, or knowledge are needed, and who has the skills we need?

- Any special needs for safety, security, sanitation, disabilities?

- What're our *Shortfalls* (anything you need to complete a project that you don't have)?

- How much money can we spend? What's our Budget?

UNRESOLVED ISSUES *(Chapter 25)*

- What do we need to know but don't?

- What do we know for sure, but the answer is unsatisfactory or unacceptable?

- What are our shortfalls, which are things we need but don't have?

- What are all the questions, unknowns, concerns, shortfalls, obstacles, or problems that could slow or stop your progress?

- Who has done this type of work before, and what were their problems, consequences, and effects?

- What are we forgetting to do?

RISK *(Chapters 31-34)*

- **Physical: (Injury, Illness, or Death)**
  - ✓ Have we inspected the site for anything that could cause injury, illness, accident, or death?
  - ✓ Have we inspected for sanitation and access for those with disabilities?

- **Security: (Cyber and Physical)**
  - ✓ For Cybersecurity: What could cause a data breach, loss of personal info or intellectual property, or a disruption of services?
  - ✓ For Physical Security: What could cause unauthorized access leading to theft, fraud, waste, abuse, or property damage?

- **Financial:**
  - ✓ What could cause financial loss or property damage?
  - ✓ What insurance do we need, and is it in-force?

- **Operational:** See Chapter 32: Risk Assessment

This page is intentionally left blank.

B
TAKE
IMMEDIATE ACTION

Do you know how to create a convincing *Decision Paper* or a *Business Case* to persuade someone to spend the money needed to move your work forward? How do you respond to unanticipated bad situations that could cause injury, property damage, security breach, or work stoppage?

Immediate Action is a proactive eight-step process used to react to any bad situation that could cause a work stoppage, property damage, a security breach, or physical injury.

When bad things happen, what do you usually do? Don't just sit there, do something! But what?

Let's drill down on the eight steps of the *Immediate Action* process.

Step 1. Assess the Situation.

Either be *on-the-scene* or in communication with someone on the ground. Assess the situation based on the facts.

Step 2. Notify Emergency Services and your boss.

If needed, call 911, and call your boss to tell him what you know.

Step 3. Consider your Options.

Look around. What's available for you to use? What should be done to stabilize the situation? What are your options? If time permits collaborate with others.

Step 4. Select the Best Option.

Select the best option, and if time permits, achieve consensus with those around you.

Step 5. Create a Plan of Action.

Create a quick mental *Plan of Action*. What's the first step? What's the second, and so forth?

Step 6. Take Decisive Action.

Using what's available, *take-charge*, and give new instructions to others. Supervise their actions.

Step 7. Reassess the Situation.

What, if anything, has changed? Did the situation stabilize, or was the problem resolved? If Yes, move to Step 8. If NO, repeat this process.

Step 8. Call your boss.

Keep your boss informed. Explain what happened, what caused it, and what you recommend be done to ensure this never happens again.

Sounds pretty easy, right? Well, let's see how it's done in the real world.

True Story

At 9 AM, two days before his company's annual Team Building Session, Bob, the Project Manager, conducted his final site inspection of the resort and was astonished by what he saw. He tried to pull into the resort, blocked by construction vehicles tearing up the parking lot. This was a disaster for Bob because he had 50 Senior Executives flying in from all over the country for this session. Fortunately, Bob knew how to take Immediate Action.

Step 1. Assess the Situation.

Bob didn't panic. He assessed the situation, took photos with his cell phone, spoke with the resort manager, and learned that a major water main had broken, which meant that the resort had no water. Bob also talked to the on-site construction manager and learned that the water main could not be repaired for another week.

Step 2. Call Emergency Services and your boss.

At 9:30 AM: Since there was no need to call 911, Bob called his boss and appraised him of the situation.

Step 3. Consider your options.

At 10 AM, Bob called a meeting of all Key Players at company headquarters to collaborate to find the best solution. Bob asked one Key Player to find another venue that could accommodate 50 people.

By 11 AM, a new venue had been found, but it was 27 miles from the airport. One problem was solved, but it created another. How will all attendees get from the airport to the resort? Someone asked, can't they just catch a cab or just rent a car at the airport? For 50 people to catch a cab or rent a car would be way too expensive.

Step 4. Select the best option.

Then someone suggested that they rent a fleet of shuttle vehicles with drivers to transport all attendees from the airport to the resort and back. They all agreed that this was the best solution.

Step 5. Create a Plan of Action.

Together they created a Plan of Action to use shuttle vehicles to accomplish the objective.

Step 6. Take Decisive Action.

Bob issued new instructions to all Key Players and supervised their actions. He assigned one Key Player to contact all attendees to let them know what happened and look for company signs at the airport directing them to shuttle vehicles rather than taking a cab or renting a vehicle. Bob also asked a second Key Player to identify and contract a shuttle company to transport all attendees. Finally, he asked everyone to meet again at 5 PM to share the status of their new assignments.

Step 7. Reassess the Situation.

At 5 PM that afternoon, Bob met with all Key Players to ensure everything was ready to move forward with a fleet of shuttle vehicles.

Step 8. Report to your boss.

At 6 PM, Bob called his boss and informed him that the problem was resolved by selecting a new site and renting a fleet of shuttle vans to drive all attendees from the airport to the hotel and back. There was no reason to recommend what needed to be done to ensure this didn't happen again. The Team Building Session went on without any further problems and turned out to be a great success.

Bob looked defeat in the eye and refused to give up,

"Snatching Victory from the Jaws of Defeat."

And you can do the same!

This page is intentionally left blank.

C
CREATE A
DECISION PAPER

Have you ever been asked to write a *Decision Paper or a Business Case*? If not, you will. This is one way your boss is preparing you for the next level.

Sometimes you'll need resources that you don't have, like people, equipment, or facilities, to solve a problem – which means spending money. When this happens, you'll need the DM's approval before moving forward. To persuade anyone to accept your recommendation, you'll need a well-written *Decision Paper,* and here's a great format.

What's the best format to use to create a Decision Paper?

1. Subject. Briefly state the subject.

2. Problem. State the problem in one sentence.

3. Recommendation. State the recommended solution in one sentence.

4. Benefits: State the expected benefits of this recommendation.

5. Key Player Comments.

A Key Player is anyone whose opinion would matter to the Decision-Maker or anyone who'll be required to support the recommendation if approved. You'll need to *Staff* your paper through all Key Players for their concurrence or non-concurrence with comments (Chapter 27). Once comments are returned, create a table showing which Key Players concurred or non-concurred with their reasons.

6. Discussion. Explain why you're recommending this solution by answering these questions.

- **What were all the solutions you considered?** Then, attach all the solutions you considered with all the Advantages and Disadvantages.
- **Why did you select this solution?**
- **What's the cost and who should pay?**

- **What's the Risk?** How probable is this risk, how severe will it be, and how can it be mitigated (Chapters 31-34). If a *Contingency Plan* is needed, add it as an enclosure (Ch 35).

- **How long will it take, and when should it be started?**

- **How long do we have before this problem becomes a crisis?**

- **What are the consequences and effects of this recommendation?** *Unintended Consequences* are outcomes that are not expected from your project. *2nd and 3rd Order Effects* deal with how your project affects others, like those in your company or your suppliers (Chapter 26).

- **What are the *Unresolved Issues*?** Attach a list of all the questions, unknowns, concerns, shortfalls, obstacles, and problems that could slow or stop your progress (Chapter 25).

- **What are all the Facts and Assumptions?** Attach a list of all the facts and assumptions you used (Appendix D).

When your paper is finished, give a Decision Briefing or provide a hard copy to the DM to gain approval. If you choose this option, ensure your paper is no more than two pages in length, with all the supporting documents attached as enclosures.

What's a Business Case?

A *Decision Paper* is also known as a *Business Case*, which is the justification to convince a Decision-Maker to accept a proposal.

A Business Case is a document that captures the reasons for initiating action.

The logic is that whenever resources are consumed, they should support a specific business need. For example, it could be a software upgrade needed to improve system performance. The *Business Case* is that a software upgrade would improve customer satisfaction, require less processing time, or reduce maintenance costs. Thus, a compelling *Business Case* captures both the quantifiable and non-quantifiable characteristics of the proposed action.

D
GATHER
ASSUMPTIONS AND FACTS

Do you know how to gather all the assumptions, facts, and the truth needed to persuade others to support you to enhance your probability of success?

By identifying the Assumptions

An ASSUMPTION is information accepted as true in the absence of facts.

However, acceptable assumptions must pass two tests.

- They must be **VALID**, which means that they're likely to be true.

- They must be **NECESSARY**, which means that they're essential to moving the work forward.

If the process can continue without the assumption, discard it. If the assumption is both valid and necessary, then treat it as a fact. Effective people continually seek to confirm their assumptions by testing. For example, if you assume that the weather won't be a problem for your company's outdoor picnic, you better have a *Contingency Plan* - just in case. Better yet, if it rains and you've reserved an outdoor picnic site with overhead cover, now you're the hero of the day.

You know what they say about assumptions, right?

Whenever you assume anything, you risk making an 'ass' out of 'u' and 'me.'

So, be careful! People aren't mind-readers. So never assume that everyone understands your expectations. It doesn't matter how much experience you have or how long you've been in your position. If you feel there's a chance of a misunderstanding, clarify all your expectations by asking better questions.

Here's an example:

"As an executive coach, one of my C-level clients shared with me his disappointment with a new VP he recently hired. He explained that he told his new VP that he expected him to really "step up" and get us to "the next level" in sales. However, after six months, he and his sales team had not met his expectations.

I asked him, "Have you defined what 'stepping up' and 'getting to the next level' mean?" My client responded, "No, why would I? With his experience, he should know what I mean." Ops!

What's an Unconscious Assumption?

Sometimes assumptions are made unconsciously. So, be careful!

Here's an example:

Bob walked into a Problem-Solving Session where one of his Direct Reports, with his entire team, tried to select the BEST vendor from two similar companies. As the process was almost over, Bob asked, "What assumptions are you making here?" Then, after a long silence, he asked the question again.

One person said, "None, we don't need any." To which Bob said, "Are you sure? Since I only see two vendors you're considering, aren't you assuming that there are only two companies that we could potentially hire to solve this problem? Are you all certain this assumption is correct?

And, what's the effect if later this assumption proves to be incorrect? What happens later when we find out that there was a third company that could have solved our problem faster and at half the cost?" Again, there was a long silence. The group had assumed there were only two potential companies, and they were wrong.

What assumptions are you making unconsciously, and what are the effects on the project if these assumptions turn out to be wrong? What's your *Contingency Plan*?

How to identify your assumptions?

To help identify your assumptions, answer these questions:

- What do I hope is true or necessary for my document to be valid?

- What assumptions are needed to move the work forward?

- What assumptions am I making unconsciously?

- If my assumption becomes false, what's my *Contingency Plan* (Chapter 35)?

Always Test your Assumptions and Vet your Facts!

By identifying the Facts

A FACT is verifiable or vetted information.

Always separate facts from opinion or speculation. According to **Colin Powell**, in his book, *It Worked for Me*, you need good information to make good decisions. Verifiable information can change over time and may not tell the whole story. So, be careful! Also, verifiable or vetted facts that come with these qualifiers should make you nervous:

"In my best judgment," or "As far as I know" or "As best as I can tell."

Here are the most important questions you need to answer:

What do you know? How do you know for sure? What do you need to know?

What do you think? What's your best hunch? What's your intuition telling you?

Always distinguish the difference. You're looking for *ground-truth*, first-hand info from people closest to the issue. The best facts are current, from a reliable source, and first-hand information rather than hearsay.

By uncovering the Truth

In solving any problem, you must uncover the root cause - the truth. The dictionary defines truth as *"that which is true or in accordance with fact or reality."*

Because of this, most people believe that all facts are true, but they're not. They're related but different. Facts can lead you to the truth, but they can also mislead you. This is because facts are what happened, while the truth is HOW and WHY it happened.

And here are a few examples.

   Fact: Mary was my best student. But the truth is that Mary was my only student.

   Fact: Sam sold nothing in May. However, the truth is that Sam was on vacation in May.

Facts without context can be misleading, and like statistics, they can be manipulated to prove or disprove just about anything. Facts can't speak for themselves. Someone else must speak for them.

Remember, nothing has meaning other than the meaning you give it. So, be careful!

What's Objective Truth?

"One of the greatest challenges in this world is to know enough about a subject to think your right, but not enough about the subject to know your wrong."

I learned from **Neal deGrasse Tyson's** *Master Class* the three categories of truth: personal, political, and objective. Objective truth is truth no matter what happens and is the truth that shapes our understanding of the universe.

"We all have susceptibility to bias. The internet is evidence of bias. And you're going to use it as evidence that you're correct? No!!!"

E
TRACK ALL
THE MOVING PARTS

Do you know how to keep track of all your moving parts to ensure that nothing *falls-through-the-cracks* to enhance your probability of success?

"Tracking" means keeping a paper or digital trail (documenting) of the most important things that keep changing.

How do you keep track of all the things that are critical to your work? Effective people know that there are many " moving parts " in business, and many lose their way - unless someone tracks them.

Here are several ways to keep track of your most important "moving parts."

By Tracking Assignments

Assignments come in two types; Assignments *Accepted* from others and Assignments *Made* to others.

Here's an example of an *Assignments Tracking Form.*

Assignments Accepted					Assignments Made			
Date	From	Action Item	DL	To	Date	DL	Checked	Status
11 May	Boss	ABC Report	19 Jun	Sue	12 May	17 Jun	2 Jun	OS

This table tracks both the assignments *accepted* from others (boss) and the assignments *made* to others. It's also a good idea to assign the *Action Item* to a Direct Report (Sue), with her deadline (DL) being a few days before your boss's deadline. This way, you have some *slack time* built in just in case something goes wrong.

For example, using this table, if your boss wants his assignment completed on May 19th, assign your Direct Report (Sue) a deadline of May 17th. This is your record of all assignments *made* for future meetings.

You can also create an *Assignment Tracking Form* for each Direct Report to use during your internal meetings. The most important thing to remember is to never trust your memory. Always document everything you've asked a Direct Report to do and add a deadline.

You can also create an *Assignment Tracking Form* for each Direct Report to use during your internal meetings. The most important thing to remember is to never trust your memory. Always document everything you've asked a Direct Report to do and add a deadline.

By Tracking Changes

Have you ever been frustrated with last-minute changes to a project? Have you ever tried to communicate a change to all Key Players, but 10% didn't get the word? Plans change, so be flexible! Make sure all Key Players know about all changes. Keep a record of who was told what, when, and how. It will come in handy later. Keep track of everyone who received the changes. Record and review these changes during your meetings.

Here's an example of a *Change Notification List*.

Change List for: _____Project (As of Aug 21, 20XX)				
Date	What Changed?	Originator?	Recipient?	How sent?
May 4	Add 12 to headcount	Bill	John	Phone
May 5	Next meeting 10 AM, not 9 AM.	Joe	Sam	Face-to-face

Notice that this table tracks the *Originator* or the source of the change, the *Recipient* or who was told about the change, and the *How Sent* or how the message was communicated.

If it's important or time-sensitive, don't use email. Many people fail to read their email for days, if at all. Many others misunderstand their email. The best means of communicating is *face-to-face* (the second is on the phone). Then, *follow-through* with a detailed email. Don't use email as your primary means of *communication.

Who else needs to know this info? Act on that answer!

By Tracking Unresolved Issues

Track all *Unresolved Issues,* including any question, unknown, concern, shortfall, obstacle, or problem that could slow or stop your progress (Chapter 25). Each issue can only be eliminated when it's both *"known for certain"* and *"acceptable to you."* If you fail to keep track of all the moving parts, expect that you'll be known as someone who doesn't have their act together.

*To learn more about **Communicating,** available at **Amazon.com,** see page 5.

F
ASSESS YOUR
ACCOUNTABILITY

Do you know what to do when your boss finds something wrong with your work?

Accountability is the acceptance of responsibility for your actions and in-actions and the obligation to report, explain, and be answerable for any adverse consequences.

Accountability is often confused with responsibility. They're related but different. *Accountability* is normally not a problem - until something goes wrong.

For example, if something goes wrong within your area of responsibility, you'll get the chance to explain what happened to your boss, and maybe his boss. Sometimes, depending on the severity of the problem, your boss won't be happy with you and may treat you badly.

Most people don't understand that, yes, responsibility and *accountability* go together; they're part of the same iceberg.

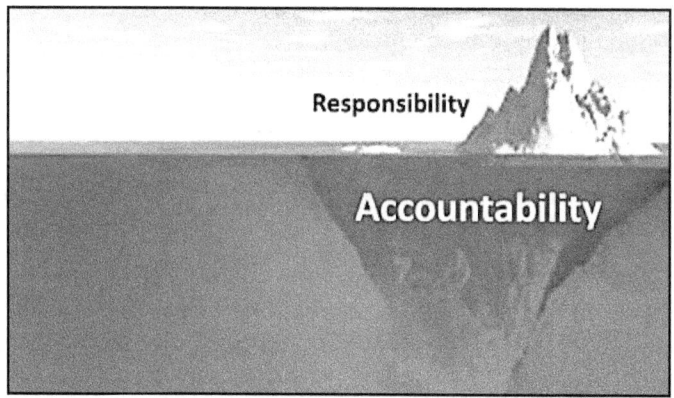

However, you can't see the *accountability* part of the iceberg because it lies hidden beneath the surface until something goes wrong.

What should you do when things go wrong?

When things go wrong for which you're responsible, your boss's job is to ask you for an explanation.

*What your boss doesn't need is for you to blame
others, make excuses, or hide the truth.*

And yes, the mistake may have been made by one of your team members - not you. But your boss doesn't care. He just wants it fixed.

Here's what your boss expects you to do:

Step 1. Step up and accept the blame!

Step 2. Investigate - what happened and what caused it to happen?

Step 3. Report the facts and recommend how it should be fixed.

Step 4. Fix it and fix it for good!

Step 5. When fixed, report the fix to your boss.

Step 6. Make sure it never happens again.

Accountability is something every boss expects from you but won't tell you until it's too late. But, unfortunately, this quality isn't something you were born with. And the only time you get to demonstrate your accountability is when things go wrong.

This also includes the actions, in-actions, and adverse consequences of those members within your charge. You're accountable to your boss for everything that happens or fails to happen within your area of responsibility.

However, *accountability* can't exist unless you know all the things for which you're responsible. For example, you can't be held *accountable* for your company's finances if your duties and responsibilities are to service rental cars.

Establish the reputation of being a good problem solver as well as a good problem finder. Your job is to help your boss find and eliminate all the obstacles that could slow or stop the achievement of his goals.

*Remember, mistakes, errors, and defects are not
a problem if they're caught and fixed before getting
in front of your boss or the customer.*

Self-Test
Are you Accountable?

Here are the most important questions to answer to assess your *accountability*.

1. Do you do what's right?

At an early age, I learned these simple lessons about accountability:

- If you lose, damage, or break something that doesn't belong to you, you need to fix it or buy it.

- If you borrow something, you need to return it in the same or better condition than you found it.

- If you back into and damage someone's car, and they're not around, you need to leave a note on their windshield with your name and phone number to help repair the damage.

- If you were mean or disrespectful to someone, you need to apologize.

2. Are you self-correcting?

A self-correcting person is someone capable of correcting himself without external help.

Part of being *accountable* is being *self-correcting*, especially when starting a new position, even if it's within the same company. Starting anything new is all about learning what you need to know as soon as possible. I'm always amazed by those who never take notes. Why do so few people take notes anymore (with your cell phone or Rocket Book)?

"A short pencil is a long memory." – Unknown.

When you have a question, write it down. Many times, the person with the correct answer won't be immediately available. If you find a term you don't understand, write it down. Later, find out what the term means. Keep a list of all your questions and terms you don't understand. This list will help later when you sponsor a new member into your team. *Self-correcting* people take notes (they don't trust their memory), write down their questions and the answers, and are not afraid to ask questions and proactively seek answers.

3. Do you live your life with no excuses?

People make excuses because it has worked for them in the past. It avoids accepting *accountability*. They're testing your limits to see how much they can get away with, and they fear the consequences of their actions or inactions.

What's the difference between a reason and an excuse?

Here's a simple rule:

Reasons are believable, understandable, and forgivable.

Excuses aren't.

Here are the commonly used excuses:

- **Denial:** Refusing to admit or acknowledge that their behavior is a problem. (Example: "I can stop swearing any time I want. My language isn't that bad.")

- **Isolation:** Removing themselves from the team area to maintain their behavior. (Example: "If I had my own office, this wouldn't be a problem.")

- **Rationalization:** Giving reasons to explain their behavior. (Example: "I screamed at him because he doesn't like me.")

- **Blaming (or Transferal):** Transferring *accountability* for their behavior to others. (Example: "I wouldn't be late all the time if my teammates treated me right.")

- **Projection:** Rejecting their feelings by ascribing them to another (Example: "Why is that stupid idiot so hostile?")

- **Minimizing or Trivialize:** Refusing to admit the effect of their behavior. (Example: "I only told one bad joke. It's not a big deal.")

They close their eyes to the destructive consequences of their unacceptable behavior, or they explain their actions in a way that saves them from having to feel. Either way, it's wrong and must be dealt with immediately.

4. Do you do your best work every day?

Here's a great story about doing your best work.

> *It's rumored that when Dr. **Henry Kissinger** was Secretary of State in the administrations of **Presidents Nixon and Ford**, he asked for a security assessment to be made of a foreign country.*
>
> *The first day, when a subordinate delivered the report, Secretary Kissinger asked, "Is this your best work?"*
>
> *The subordinate thought for a second and walked out of the office. The second day, the subordinate returned with the report, and Kissinger asked the same question. The subordinate again thought for a moment and walked back out of the office.*
>
> *On the third day, the subordinate returned, and Kissinger asked for the third time, "Is this your best work?" This time the subordinate said, "Yes." Kissinger then responded, "Good, now I'll read it."*

I share this story to highlight that there are no shortcuts to success. Your success will always be linked to *"doing your best work."* Do you do your best work every day? Would your boss agree?

5. Are you proactive?

Another thing that contributes to your effectiveness and success at work is your ability to be proactive.

A proactive person identifies and prevents potential problems by causing things to happen rather than reacting to them after they happen.

Proactive people:

- Identify potential pre-problems (Chapter 4) before they become a problem and problems before they become a crisis.

- Anticipate their boss's and customer's needs and expectations (Chapter 7).

- Use Preventive Actions (Chapter 4) to identify and resolve all Pre-Problems.

- Take-charge (Chapter 21) and produce order in the midst of chaos.

- Use collaborative problem solving to build consensus (Chapter 27) and resolve Unresolved Issues (Chapter 25)

- Take Immediate Action (Appendix B) and don't wait to be told what to do.

- Anticipate Unintended Consequences and 2d and 3d Order Effects (Chapter 26)

- Manage risk (Chapters 31-33) and make things happen the right way the first time.

6. Do you make recommendations to your boss to make things better?

Your job is to help your boss achieve his goals. What do you do when you find a problem or an improvement that could make things better? Do you create a *Decision Paper* or a *Business Case* (Appendix C) to make it happen?

I've often written Decision Papers through my boss to his boss because my boss didn't have the funding to make it happen. As shown below, the Decision Paper was addressed "To," my boss's boss, "Thru," my boss.

To: My boss's boss.

Thru: My boss.

From: Me

My boss would then initial and write "Approved" next to the "Thru" line above and send it to his boss for final approval. This process helped my boss move the work forward.

7. Do you know how to apologize with remorse?

Why is it so hard to say you're sorry or admit a mistake? The answer is simple; you're letting your fear and pride get in your way of doing the right thing.

When you hurt someone's feelings, or your behavior was unacceptable, have the moral courage to apologize, say you're sorry, what you're sorry for, offer no excuse, and don't do it again.

Why no excuses? Making excuses diminishes your sincerity and makes you sound like you're trying to hide behind your excuse. You're human, and humans make mistakes.

Express your sincere remorse, not guilt. Guilt is acknowledging your unacceptable behavior, while remorse is regretting your actions and taking steps to undo the damage.

When your finish, look down, say nothing, and wait for a response. The other person doesn't have to forgive you, but you need to forgive yourself and move forward.

Most importantly, there's no excuse
for unacceptable behavior.

Guilt leads to destructive tendencies, while remorse leads to constructive actions. To be remorseful, you must accept the guilt first.

When you make a mistake, have the moral courage
to admit it, fix it, and learn from it.

If you cannot answer these questions with a strong YES, you need to reassess your *accountability*. Effective people take this assessment annually and fix what needs to be fixed.

This page is intentionally left blank.

ACKNOWLEDGMENTS

"Many people will walk in and out of your life, but only true friends will leave footprints in your heart."
- Eleanor Roosevelt

I'd like to recognize those with whom I've had the pleasure of serving, whose effectiveness and character I vividly recall, many of whom are not here today to tell their story.

For my military career, I thank Betty McIntee, Edward J. Murphy (my Dad), Dale R. Nelson, Geoffrey "Jeff" Prosch, Craig "Randy" Rutler, Dave Wagner, John Andrews, John "The Bear" Warren, John "Jack" Costello, Dan Labin, and Ron Nicholl for their example of effectiveness.

For my coaching career, I thank Tony Robbins, Bernard Haldane, Jack Bissell, Len Drew, Wayne McCullum, Bob Schrier, John Hurtig, and Bob Gerberg for their mentoring and coaching.

Special thanks to my long-time mentor and friend, Joyce Kuntz, who encouraged me to write this Playbook. After leaving the US Military, Joyce was my first and best boss when I joined her consulting firm in Seattle years ago. Unfortunately, Joyce is gone now, but her legacy lives on in this Playbook.

"I must be able to say with sincerity that to see things differently is a strength, not a weakness, in my relationship with others."
- Joyce Kuntz

I thank Joyce's husband, Ed Kuntz, who turned out to be the man who brought me to Seattle from Kansas City to start my incredible second career as an Executive Coach.

And finally, I thank my soulmate and wife, ***Diana,*** for her love, encouragement, and understanding throughout this process.

When I count my blessings, I always count her twice.

This page is intentionally left blank.

ABOUT THE AUTHOR

"I expect to pass through this world but once; any good thing therefore that I can do, or any kindness that I can show to any fellow creature, let me do it now; let me not defer or neglect it, for I shall not pass this way again."
- Stephan Grelle

Ed Murphy considers himself lucky. From age 7, he knew what he wanted to be when he grew up. He wanted to be a Soldier. So after graduating from High School, he joined the US Army and found himself in Basic Training and Advanced Infantry Training at Fort Dix, New Jersey.

A year later, Ed became a Cadet at the United States Military Academy at West Point. In 1970, he graduated as a 2d Lieutenant headed to Airborne and Ranger School, then off to Viet Nam for a year.

In 1978, Ed returned to West Point to teach Military Science and earned an MS from LIU in night school. During his tenure as a Battalion Commander in West Germany, his greatest achievement was helping 1400 soldiers begin a college education. He wanted to give his soldiers something of real value - something that no one could ever take away. After 23 years as a US Army Officer, he retired in 1993.

For his second career, with a little help from *Tony Robbins*, he became an Executive Coach. Then, for the next 21 years, he worked for four of the largest career development and outplacement companies in America, from Seattle, San Diego, Kansas City, and Phoenix.

In 2012, Ed retired a second time and decided to document everything he learned from those he most admired during his 50+ years in the US Military as an Army Officer and Corporate America as an Executive Coach.

In 2014, he began writing books for Amazon and Kindle dedicated to providing the best-in-class wisdom, knowledge, and advice to help others maximize their true career potential by becoming more effective and successful at work and in life.

Today, Ed considers himself blessed to get to live in Phoenix, AZ. He enjoys writing, eating sushi, genealogy, and watching movies with family, friends, and his best friend and wife, ***Diana.***

CONCLUSION

Congratulations!

And thank you for joining us on this *Journey of Discovery*.

As promised, you now have an *Organizing Guide* to add to your professional library - the one I never had.

Every effective boss needs effective followers who can consistently produce excellent results and add value to those who helped produce those results.

You now have the most actionable *Organizing Skills* you were never taught in school or college to support you throughout your career.

Now it's your turn to apply and share this new knowledge to add greater value to your boss and all those with whom you serve.

These are the essential *Best Practices* I've learned over the past 50 years to help you become far more effective and successful than you were yesterday.

As always, I wish you great success.

Never STOP Learning!

Ed

Founder of *The Effectiveness Institute*

email: ed.murphy77@gmail.com

PS: Also, if you feel this information could help someone else, please let them know. If it turns out to make a difference in their life, they'll be forever grateful to you, as will I.

Stop wishing you were better and do something about it today.

www.ingramcontent.com/pod-product-compliance
Lightning Source LLC
Chambersburg PA
CBHW051914170526
45168CB00001B/386